The Proverbs of Solomon

Practical Instructions for Successful Living

Bridgett Muldrow

The Proverbs of Solomon

A daily cup of spiritual "tea" to guide you through the year.

While the publisher has made every attempt to release correct addresses and contact information at the time of this publication, the publisher assumes no responsibility for errors or changes that come about after the publish date.

All rights reserved. No part of this book may be reproduced, scanned, or distributed in any printed or electronic forms existing now or in the future without written permission from the publisher. For information regarding permission, please write to:

Galaxy Arizona

www.galaxyarizona.com

Please help in the fight against piracy of

copyrighted materials.

Purchase only authorized editions.

© 2023 Galaxy Arizona. All rights reserved. Published 2023.

Printed in the United States of America.

Scripture quotations marked (NLT) are taken from the Holy Bible, New Living Translation, Copyright ©1996. Used by permission of Tyndale House Publishers, Inc., Wheaton, Illinois 60189. All Rights Reserved

Dedication

I want to dedicate this book to my 6 Glamchildren:

Victor F. Holmes III

Braelynn Clemons

Max F. Holmes

Jadira Clemons

Naomi & Nasir Holmes

Acknowledgement

My beloved parents William "Ted" Muldrow and Almond (Martin) Muldrow are now both in Heaven together. My mother was truly a Virtuous woman, and my father was my Zacharias, keeping me safe and protecting me.

William, my big brother, thanks for finally making me an Auntie. Carl, my little brother, you remind us so much of Dad, it's like he never left. My beautiful children: Bianca, "The Star," my first-born daughter, use your natural born gifts to entertain people. Victor, "The Prize Fighter," my first-born son, use God as your Personal trainer and you'll be "Victor"ious. Wanya, "The Cool Nerd," my second born son, I pray you keep your humble spirit, you truly are a sweetheart. Elijah, my third born son, "Little Einstein," you truly are an intelligent child.

INTRODUCTION

The Book of Proverbs was written mostly by Solomon (Prov.1:1 & 10:1 claim Solomon as the author of the bulk of the book.): Agur, son of Jakeh; King Lemuel (an oracle, wise statements, taught to him by his mother.) and many others. The book of Proverbs is believed to have been written in the 10th Century B.C. and later.

The book of Proverbs contains practical instructions for successful living. It teaches that there is special wisdom revealed by God as well as innate wisdom or common sense, and both must play a part in daily life. This book is a collection of practical wisdom from many centuries, and it deals with such diverse matters as:

Children, Discipline, Family, Friends, Humility, Idleness, Immoral Women, Justice, Poverty, Pride, Sin, Vengeance, Virtuous Wife, and Work (Just to name a few). The theme of Proverbs is stated in 1:7: "Fear of the LORD is the beginning of knowledge." Only fools despise wisdom and discipline. This is to say that only when a person trusts in God will he or she be truly wise. Human wisdom is fine and necessary, but no matter how skilled a person might be, without a humble willingness to learn from God, he or she will end up in trouble. The book also teaches that even everyday life is sacred. God is concerned with all of life, and he has shown us how to live well.

Defining Proverbs:

What Exactly Does Proverbs Mean?

Well, I looked up the word proverbs in the dictionary, but not in just any dictionary. I looked the word up in the Compact Bible Dictionary, which is considered to be one of the most comprehensive resources for biblical information available today. Proverbs mean a pithy saying, comparison, or question. (I Kings 4:32: Proverbs 1:1,6:Eccl. 12:9). A proverb may be a snatch of poetry, showing parallelism of structure, a sharp question; a pregnant sentence; or a very brief story. Felicity of expression ensure its long preservation and wide currency through oral transmission, even after it is fixed in literary, written form. Now to, define the words underlined within the definition. (Don't you just love it when the Definer of a definition uses words within the definition that you have to also look up in order to understand the definition of the word you are trying to define.) Oh! I said a mouthful just then.

- **Pithy:** is an adjective meaning like or full of essence, importance, concise and full of meaning.
- **Felicity:** is a noun meaning happiness; apt and pleasing style in writing, speech, etc...
- **Parallelism**: is a noun meaning the quality or state of being compared or similar.
- **Pregnant:** is an adjective meaning significant, meaningful.

Filled with significance and meaning.

The book of Proverbs is comprised, made up of 31 chapters containing 903 verses. It is divided into seven segments:

I. The Purpose of Proverbs 1:1-1:7
II. The Search for Wisdom 1:8-9:18
III. Specific Proverbs of Solomon 10:1-24:34
IV. Proverbs of Solomon copied by the Advisors of King Hezekiah of Judah 25:1-29:27
V. The Words, Sayings of Agur 30:1-33
VI. The Words, Sayings of King Lemuel 31:1-9
VII. The Virtuous Wife – A Wife of Noble Character 31:10 –31:31

Max Anders, author of 30 Days to Understanding the Bible in 15 Minutes a Day! States in chapter thirteen: Proverbs is one of the five Poetical Books in the Old Testament. He also stated that the Poetical Books fall into three major types of poetry, within which the poets used a number of different literary techniques to communicate God's Message. The three major types of Hebrew poetry are:

1. Lyric poetry: to be accompanied by music, like a song.
2. Instructional poetry: to teach principles of living through pithy maxims. (concise rule)
3. Dramatic poetry: a narrative that tells a story in poetic form.

Proverbs, this "Instructional poetry" is written in short, pithy, concise maxims – rules of conduct, focusing on one's relationship to God and others – money, morals, speech, industry, honesty, etc. The message is that a life of wisdom and righteousness should preempt a life of foolishness and unrighteousness.

Reading the Word of God is like medicine to the mind, body, soul, and spirit. In order for the medicine to make you feel better, you must take the right dosage at the right time and for the prescribed period of time; so that you may go back to work (God's work, that is.) God did not want to overwhelm you, so he put it in my heart to focus on the Specific Proverbs of Solomon, beginning at chapter 10:1 to chapter 24:34, for my first handbook.

I suggest that you read a page per day and really try to internalize God's Words of Wisdom to us and begin to follow His guidance.

The pages have been numbered by the month and date; your first page should be the first day you begin reading the book. (for example: If you begin reading the book on February 26th - that is your first page. You read a page daily until December 31st, then on January 1st, you start again.

May God bless you with knowledge, wisdom and understanding of His Word and of His Way.

Peace and Blessings from Your Sister – in – Faith, Sister **Bridgett Muldrow**

Proverbs of Solomon
Practical Instructions for Successful Living

January 1

"A Wise Child Brings Joy To A Father, A Foolish Child Brings Grief To A Mother."

(Prov.10:1) NLT

"A Wise Son Maketh A Glad Father: But A Foolish Son Is The Heaviness Of His Mother"

(Prov.10:1) KJV

Proverbs of Solomon
Practical Instructions for Successful Living

January 2

"Ill-Gotten Gain Has No Lasting Value, But Right Living Can Save Your Life."

(Prov.10:2) NLT

"Treasures Of Wickedness Profit Nothing: But Righteousness Delivereth From Death."

(Prov.10:2) KJV

Proverbs of Solomon
Practical Instructions for Successful Living

January 3

"The LORD Will Not Let The Godly Starve To Death, But He Refuses To Satisfy The Cravings Of The Wicked."

(Prov.10:3) NLT

"The LORD Will Not Suffer The Soul Of The Righteous To Famish: But He Casteth Away The Substance Of The Wicked."

(Prov.10:3) KJV

Proverbs of Solomon
Practical Instructions for Successful Living

January 4

"Lazy People Are Soon Poor; Hard Workers Get Rich."

(Prov.10:4) NLT

"He Becometh Poor That Dealeth With A Slack Hand: But The Hand Of The Diligent Maketh Rich."

(Prov.10:4) KJV

Proverbs of Solomon
Practical Instructions for Successful Living

January 5

"A Wise Youth Works Hard All Summer: A Youth Who Sleeps Away The Hour Of Opportunity Brings Shame."

(Prov.10:5) NLT

"He That Gathereth In Summer Is A Wise Son: But He That Sleepeth In Harvest Is A Son That Causeth Shame."

(Prov.10:5) KJV

Proverbs of Solomon
Practical Instructions for Successful Living

January 6

"The Godly Are Showered With Blessings: Evil People Cover Up Their Harmful Intentions."

(Prov.10:6) NLT

"Blessings Are Upon The Head Of The Just: But Violence Covereth The Mouth Of The Wicked."

(Prov.10:6) KJV

Proverbs of Solomon
Practical Instructions for Successful Living

January 7

"We All Have Happy Memories Of The Godly, But The Name Of A Wicked Person Rots Away."

(Prov.10:7) NLT

"The Memory Of The Just Is Blessed: But The Name Of The Wicked Shall Rot."

(Prov.10:7) KJV

Proverbs of Solomon
Practical Instructions for Successful Living

January 8

"The Wise Are Glad To Be Instructed, But Babbling Fools Fall Flat On Their Faces."

(Prov.10:8) NLT

"The Wise In Heart Will Receive Commandments: But A Prating Fool Shall Fall."

(Prov.10:8) KJV

Proverbs of Solomon
Practical Instructions for Successful Living

January 9

"People With Integrity Have A Firm Footing, But Those Who Follow Crooked Paths Will Slip And Fall."

(Prov10:9) NLT

"He That Walketh Uprightly Walketh Surely: But He That Perverteth His Ways Shall Be Known."

(Prov.10:9) KJV

Proverbs of Solomon
Practical Instructions for Successful Living

January 10

"People Who Wink At Wrong Cause Trouble, But A Bold Reproof Promotes Peace."

(Prov.10:10) NLT

"He That Winketh With The Eye Causeth Sorrow: But A Prating Fool Shall Fall."

(Prov.10:10) KJV

Proverbs of Solomon
Practical Instructions for Successful Living

January 11

"The Words Of The Godly Lead To Life; Evil People Cover Up Their Harmful Intentions."

(Prov.10:11) NLT

"The Mouth Of A Righteous Man Is A Well Of Life: But Violence Covereth The Mouth Of The Wicked."

(Prov.10:11) KJV

Proverbs of Solomon
Practical Instructions for Successful Living

January 12

"Hatred Stirs Up Quarrels, But Love Covers All Offenses."

(Prov.10:12) NLT

"Hatred Stirreth Up Strifes: But Love Covereth All Sins."

(Prov.10:12) KJV

Proverbs of Solomon
Practical Instructions for Successful Living

January 13

"Wise Words Come From The Lips Of People With Understanding, But Fools Will Be Punished With A Rod."

(Prov.10:13) NLT

"In The Lips Of Him That Hath Understanding Wisdom Is Found: But A Rod Is For the Back Of Him That Is Void Of Understanding."

(Prov.10:13) KJV

Proverbs of Solomon
Practical Instructions for Successful Living

January 14

"Wise People Treasure Knowledge, But The Babbling Of A Fool Invites Trouble."

(Prov.10:14) NLT

"Wise Men Lay Up Knowledge: But The Mouth Of The Foolish Is Near Destruction."

(Prov.10:14) KJV

Proverbs of Solomon
Practical Instructions for Successful Living

January 15

"The Wealth Of The Rich Is their Fortress; The Poverty Of The Poor Is Their Calamity."

(Prov.10:15) NLT

"The Rich Man's Wealth Is His Strong City: The Destruction Of The Poor Is Their Poverty."

(Prov.10:15) KJV

Proverbs of Solomon
Practical Instructions for Successful Living

January 16

"The Earnings Of The Godly Enhance Their Lives, But Evil People Squander Their Money On Sin."

(Prov.10:1) NLT

"The Labour Of The Righteous Tendeth To Life: The Fruit Of The Wicked To Sin."

(Prov.10:16) KJV

Proverbs of Solomon
Practical Instructions for Successful Living

January 17

"People Who Accept Correction Are On The Pathway To Life, But Those Who Ignore It Will Lead Others Astray."

(Prov.10:17) NLT

"He Is In The Way Of Life That Keepeth Instruction: But He That Refuseth Reproof Erreth."

(Prov.10:17) KJV

Proverbs of Solomon
Practical Instructions for Successful Living

January 18

"To Hide Hatred Is To Be A Liar; To Slander Is To Be A Fool."

(Prov.10:18) NLT

"He That Hideth Hatred With Lying Lips, And He That Uttereth A Slander Is A Fool."

(Prov.10:18) KJV

Proverbs of Solomon
Practical Instructions for Successful Living

January 19

"Don't Talk Too Much, For It Fosters Sin. Be Sensible And Turn Off The Flow!"

(Prov.10:19) NLT

"In The Multitude Of Words There Wanteth Not Sin: But He That Refraineth His Lips Is Wise."

(Prov.10:19) KJV

Proverbs of Solomon
Practical Instructions for Successful Living

January 20

"The Words Of The Godly Are Like Sterling Silver: The Heart Of A Fool Is Worthless."

(Prov.10:20) NLT

"The Tongue Of The Just Is As Choice Silver: The Heart Of The Wicked Is Little Worth."

(Prov.10:20) KJV

Proverbs of Solomon
Practical Instructions for Successful Living

January 21

"The Godly Give Good Advice, But Fools Are Destroyed By Their Lack Of Common Sense."

(Prov.10:21)NLT

"The Lips Of The Righteous Feed Many: But Fools Die For The Want Of Wisdom."

(Prov.10:21) KJV

Proverbs of Solomon
Practical Instructions for Successful Living

January 22

"The Blessing Of The LORD Makes A Person Rich, And He Adds No Sorrow With It."

(Prov.10:22) NLT

"The Blessing Of The LORD, It Maketh Rich, And He Addeth No Sorrow With It."

(Prov.10:22) KJV

Proverbs of Solomon
Practical Instructions for Successful Living

January 23

"Doing Wrong Is Fun For A Fool, While Wise Conduct Is The Pleasure To The Wise."

(Prov.10:23) NLT

"It Is As Sport To A Fool To Do Mischief: But A Man Of Understanding Hath Wisdom."

(Prov.10:23) KJV

Proverbs of Solomon
Practical Instructions for Successful Living

January 24

"The Fears of the Wicked Will All Come True; So Will The Hopes Of The Godly."

(Prov.10:24) NLT

"The Fear of the Wicked, It Shall Come Upon Him: But The Desire Of The Righteous Shall Be Granted."

(Prov.10:24) KJV

Proverbs of Solomon
Practical Instructions for Successful Living

January 25

"Disaster Strikes Like A Cyclone, Whirling The Wicked Away, But The Godly Have A Lasting Foundation."

(Prov.10:25) NLT

"As The Whirlwind Passeth, So Is The Wicked No More, But The Righteous Is An Everlasting Foundation."

(Prov.10:25) KJV

Proverbs of Solomon
Practical Instructions for Successful Living

January 26

"Lazy People Are A Pain To Their Employer. They Are Like Smoke In The Eyes Or Vinegar That Sets The Teeth On Edge."

(Prov.10:26) NLT

"As Vinegar To The Teeth, And As Smoke To The Eyes, So Is The Sluggard To Them That Send Him."

(Prov.10:26) KJV

Proverbs of Solomon
Practical Instructions for Successful Living

January 27

"Fear Of The LORD Lengthens One's Life, But The Years Of The Wicked Are Cut Short."

(Prov.10:27) NLT

"The Fear Of The LORD Prolongeth Days: But The Years Of The Wicked Shall Be Shortened."

(Prov.10:27) KJV

Proverbs of Solomon
Practical Instructions for Successful Living

January 28

"The Hopes Of The Godly Result In Happiness, But The Expectations Of The Wicked Are All In Vain."

(Prov.10:28) NLT

"The Hope Of The Righteous Shall Be Gladness: But The Expectation Of The Wicked Shall Perish."

(Prov.10:28) KJV

Proverbs of Solomon
Practical Instructions for Successful Living

January 29

"The LORD Protects The Upright But Destroys The Wicked."

(Prov.10:29) NLT

"The Way Of The LORD Is Strength To The Upright: But Destruction Shall Be To The Workers Of Iniquity."

(Prov.10:29) KJV

Proverbs of Solomon
Practical Instructions for Successful Living

January 30

"The Godly Will Never Be Disturbed, But The Wicked Will Be Removed From The Land."

(Prov.10:30) NLT

"The Righteous Shall Never Be Removed: But The Wicked Shall Not Inhabit The Earth."

(Prov.10:30) KJV

Proverbs of Solomon
Practical Instructions for Successful Living

January 31

"The Godly Person Gives Wise Advice, But The Tongue That Deceives Will Be Cut Off."

(Prov.10:31) NLT

"The Mouth Of The Just Bringeth Forth Wisdom: But The Froward Tongue Shall Be Cut Out."

(Prov.10:31) KJV

Proverbs of Solomon
Practical Instructions for Successful Living

February 1

"The Godly Speak Words That Are Helpful, But The Wicked Speak Only What Is Corrupt."

(Prov.10:32) NLT

"The Lips Of The Righteous Know What Is Acceptable: But The Mouth Of The Wicked Speaketh Frowardness."

(Prov.10:32) KJV

Proverbs of Solomon
Practical Instructions for Successful Living

February 2

"The LORD Hates Cheating, But He Delights In Honesty."

(Prov.11:1) NLT

"A False Balance Is Abomination To The LORD: But A Just Weight Is His Delight."

(Prov.11:1) KJV

Proverbs of Solomon
Practical Instructions for Successful Living

February 3

"Good People Are Guided By Their Honesty; Treacherous People Are Destroyed By Their Dishonesty."

(Prov.11:3) NLT

"The Integrity Of The Upright Shall Guide Them: But The Perverseness Of Transgressors Shall Destroy Them."

(Prov.11:3) KJV

Proverbs of Solomon
Practical Instructions for Successful Living

February 4

"Riches Won't Help On The Day Of Judgement, But Right Living Is Safeguard Against Death."

(Prov.11:4) NLT

"Riches Profit Not In The Day Of Wrath: But Righteousness Delivereth From Death."

(Prov.11:4) KJV

Proverbs of Solomon
Practical Instructions for Successful Living

February 5

"The Godly Are Directed By Their Honesty; The Wicked Fall Beneath Their Load Of Sin."

(Prov.11:5) NLT

"The Righteousness Of The Perfect Shall Direct His Way: But The Wicked Shall Fall By Their Own Wickedness."

(Prov.11:5) KJV

Proverbs of Solomon
Practical Instructions for Successful Living

February 6

"The Godliness Of Good People Rescues Them; The Ambition Of Treacherous People Traps Them."

(Prov.11:6) NLT

"The Righteousness Of The Upright Shall Deliver Them: But Transgressors Shall Be Taken In Their Own Naughtiness."

(Prov.11:6) KJV

Proverbs of Solomon
Practical Instructions for Successful Living

February 7

"When The Wicked Die, Their Hopes All Perish, For They Rely On Their Own Feeble Strength."

(Prov.11:7) NLT

"When A Wicked Man Dieth, His Expectation Shall Perish: And The Hope Of Unjust Men Perisheth."

(Prov.11:7) KJV

Proverbs of Solomon
Practical Instructions for Successful Living

February 8

"God Rescues The Godlly From Danger, But He Lets The Wicked Fall Into Trouble."

(Prov.11:8) NLT

"The Righteous Is Delivered Out Of Trouble, And The Wicked Cometh In His Stead."

(Prov.11:8) KJV

Proverbs of Solomon
Practical Instructions for Successful Living

February 9

"Evil Words Destroy One's Friends; Wise Discernment Rescues The Godly."

(Prov.11:9) NLT

"An Hypocrite With His Mouth Destroyeth His Neighbour: But Through Knowledge Shall The Just Be Delivered."

(Prov.11:9) KJV

Proverbs of Solomon
Practical Instructions for Successful Living

February 10

"The Whole City Celebrates When The Godly Succeed; They Shout For Joy When The Godless Die."

(Prov.11:10) NLT

"When It Goeth Well With The Righteous, The City Rejoiceth: And When The Wicked Perish, There Is Shouting."

(Prov.11:10) KJV

Proverbs of Solomon
Practical Instructions for Successful Living

February 11

"Upright Citizens Bless A City And Make It Prosper, But The Talk Of The Wicked Tears It Apart."

(Prov.11:11) NLT

"By The Blessing Of The Upright The City Is Exalted: But It Is Overthrown By The Mouth Of The Wicked."

(Prov.11:11) KJV

Proverbs of Solomon
Practical Instructions for Successful Living

February 12

"It Is Foolish To Belittle A Neighbor; A Person With Good Sense Remains Silent."

(Prov.11:12) NLT

"He That Is Void Of Wisdom Despiseth His Neighbour: But A Man Of Understanding Holdeth His Peace."

(Prov.11:12) KJV

Proverbs of Solomon
Practical Instructions for Successful Living

February 13

"A Gossip Goes Around Revealing Secrets, But Those Who Are Trustworthy Can Keep A Confidence."

(Prov.11:13) NLT

"A Talebearer Revealeth Secrets: But He That Is Of A Faithful Spirit Concealeth The Matter."

(Prov.11:13)KJV

Proverbs of Solomon
Practical Instructions for Successful Living

February 14

"Without Wise Leadership, A Nation Falls; With Many Counselors, There Is Safety."

(Prov.11:14) NLT

"Where No Counsel Is, The People Fall: But In The Multitude Of Counsellors There Is Safety."

(Prov.11:14) KJV

Proverbs of Solomon
Practical Instructions for Successful Living

February 15

"Guaranteeing A Loan For A Stranger Is Dangerous; It Is Better to Refuse Than To Suffer Later."

(Prov.11:15) NLT

"He That Is Surety For A Stranger Shall Smart For It: And He That Hateth Suretiship Is Sure"

(Prov.11:15) KJV

Proverbs of Solomon
Practical Instructions for Successful Living

February 16

"Beautiful Women Obtain Wealth, And Violent Men Get Rich."

(Prov.11:16) NLT

"A Gracious Woman Obtain Wealth, And Strong Men Retain Riches"

(Prov.11:16) KJV

Proverbs of Solomon
Practical Instructions for Successful Living

February 17

"Your Own Soul Is Nourished When You Are Kind, But You Destroy Yourself When You Are Cruel."

(Prov.11:17) NLT

"The Merciful Man Doeth Good To His Own Soul: But He That Is Cruel Troubleth His Own Flesh."

(Prov.11:17) KJV

Proverbs of Solomon
Practical Instructions for Successful Living

February 18

"Evil People Get Rich For The Moment, But The Reward Of The Godly Will Last."

(Prov.11:18) NLT

"The Wicked Worketh A Deceitful Work: But To Him That Showeth Righteousness Shall Be A Sure Reward."

(Prov.11:18) KJV

Proverbs of Solomon
Practical Instructions for Successful Living

February 19

"Godly People Find Life; Evil People Find Death."

(Prov.11:19) NLT

"As Righteousness Tendeth To Life: So He That Pursueth Evil Pursueth It To His Own Death."

(Prov.11:19) KJV

Proverbs of Solomon
Practical Instructions for Successful Living

February 20

"The LORD Hates People With Twisted Hearts, But He Delights In Those Who Have Integrity."

(Prov.11:20) NLT

"They That Are Of A Froward Heart Are Abomination To The LORD: But Such As Are Upright In Their Way Are His Delight."

(Prov.11:20) KJV

Proverbs of Solomon
Practical Instructions for Successful Living

February 21

"You Can Be Sure That Evil People Will Be Punished, But The Children Of The Godly Will Go Free."

(Prov.11:21) NLT

"Though Hand Join In Hand, The Wicked Shall Not Be Unpunished: But The Seed Of The Righteous Shall Be Delivered."

(Prov.11:21) KJV

Proverbs of Solomon
Practical Instructions for Successful Living

February 22

"A Woman Who Is Beautiful But Lacks Discretion Is Like A Gold Ring In A Pig's Snout."

(Prov.11:22) NLT

"As A Jewel Of Gold In A Swine's Snout, So Is A Fair Woman Which Is Without Discretion."

(Prov.11:22) KJV

Proverbs of Solomon
Practical Instructions for Successful Living

February 23

"The Godly Can Look Forward To Happiness, While The Wicked Can Expect Only Wrath."

(Prov.11:23) NLT

"The Desire Of The Righteous Is Only Good: But the Expectation Of The Wicked Is Wrath."

(Prov.11:23) KJV

Proverbs of Solomon
Practical Instructions for Successful Living

February 24

"It Is Possible To Give Freely And Become More Wealthy, But those Who Are Stingy Will Lose Everything"

(Prov.11:24) NLT

"There Is That Scattereth And Yet Increaseth; And There Is That Withholdeth More Than Is Meet, But It Tendeth To Poverty."

(Prov.11:24) KJV

Proverbs of Solomon
Practical Instructions for Successful Living

February 25

"The Generous Prosper And Are Satisfied; Those Who Refresh Others Will Themselves Be Refreshed."

(Prov.11:25) NLT

"The Liberal Soul Shall Be Made Fat: And He That Watereth Shall Be Watered Also Himself."

(Prov.11:25) KJV

Proverbs of Solomon
Practical Instructions for Successful Living

February 26

"People Curse Those Who Hold Their Grain For Higher Prices, But They Bless The One Who Sells to Them In Their Time Of Need."

(Prov.11:26) NLT

"He That Withholdeth Corn, The People Shall Curse Him: But Blessing Shall Be Upon The Head Of Him That Selleth It."

(Prov.11:26) KJV

Proverbs of Solomon
Practical Instructions for Successful Living

February 27

"If You Search For Good, You Will Find Favor; But If You Search For Evil, It Will Find You!"

(Prov.11:27) NLT

"He That Diligently Seeketh Good Procureth Favour: But He That Seeketh Mischief, It Shall Come Unto Him."

(Prov.11:27) KJV

Proverbs of Solomon
Practical Instructions for Successful Living

February 28

"Trust In Your Money And Down You Go! But The Godly Flourish Like Leaves In Spring."

(Prov.11:28) NLT

"He That Trusteth In His Riches Shall Fall: But The Righteous Shall Flourish As A Branch."

(Prov.11:28) KJV

Proverbs of Solomon
Practical Instructions for Successful Living

February 29

"Those Who Bring Trouble On Their Families Inherit Only The Wind. The Fool Will Be A Servant To The Wise."

(Prov.11:29) NLT

"He That Troubleth His Own House Shall Inherit The Wind: And The Fool Shall Be Servant To The Wise Of Heart"

(Prov.11:29) KJV

Proverbs of Solomon
Practical Instructions for Successful Living

March 1

"The Godly Are Like Trees That Bear Life-Giving Fruit, And Those Who Save Lives Are Wise."

(Prov.11:30) NLT

"The Fruit Of The Righteous Is A Tree Of Life; And He That Winneth Souls Is Wise."

(Prov.11:30) KJV

Proverbs of Solomon
Practical Instructions for Successful Living

March 2

"If The Righteous Are Rewarded Here On Earth, How Much More True That The Wicked And The Sinner Will Get What They Deserve."

(Prov.11:31) NLT

"Behold, The Righteous Shall Be Recompensed In The Earth: Much More The Wicked And The Sinner."

(Prov.11:31) KJV

Proverbs of Solomon
Practical Instructions for Successful Living

March 3

"To Learn You Must Love Discipline; It Is Stupid To Hate Correction."

(Prov.12:1) NLT

"Whoso Loveth Instruction Loveth Knowledge: But He That Hateth Reproof Is Brutish."

(Prov.12:1) KJV

Proverbs of Solomon
Practical Instructions for Successful Living

March 4

"The LORD Approves Of Those Who Are Good, But He Condemns Those Who Plan Wickedness."

(Prov.12:2) NLT

"A Good Man Obtaineth Favour Of The LORD: But A Man Of Wicked Devices Will He Condemn."

(Prov.12:2) KJV

Proverbs of Solomon
Practical Instructions for Successful Living

March 5

"Wickedness Never Brings Stability; Only The Godly Have Deep Roots."

(Prov.12:3) NLT

"A Man Shall Not Be Established By Wickedness: But The Root Of The Righteous Shall Not Be Moved."

(Prov.12:3) KJV

Proverbs of Solomon
Practical Instructions for Successful Living

March 6

"A Worthy Wife Is Her Husband's Joy And Crown; A Shameful Wife Saps His Strength."

(Prov.12:4) NLT

"A Virtuous Woman Is A Crown To Her Husband: But She That Maketh Ashamed Is As Rottenness In His Bones."

(Prov.12:4) KJV

Proverbs of Solomon
Practical Instructions for Successful Living

March 7

"The Plans Of The Godly Are Just; The Advice Of The Wicked Is Treacherous."

(Prov.12:5) NLT

"The Thoughts Of The Righteous Are Right: But The Counsels Of The Wicked Are Deceit."

(Prov.12:5) KJV

Proverbs of Solomon
Practical Instructions for Successful Living

March 8

"The Words Of The Wicked Are Like A Murderous Ambush, But The Words Of The Godly Saves Lives."

(Prov.12:6) NLT

"The Words Of The Wicked Are To Lie In Wait For Blood: But The Mouth Of The Upright Shall Deliver Them."

(Prov.12:6) KJV

Proverbs of Solomon
Practical Instructions for Successful Living

March 9

"The Wicked Perish And Are Gone, But The Children Of The Godly Stand Firm."

(Prov.12:7) NLT

"The Wicked Are Overthrown, And Are Not: But The House Of The Righteous Shall Stand."

(Prov.12:7) KJV

Proverbs of Solomon
Practical Instructions for Successful Living

March 10

"Everyone Admires A Person With Good Sense, But A Warped Mind Is Despised."

(Prov.12:8) NLT

"A Man Shall Be Commended According To His Wisdom: But He That Is Of A Perverse Heart Shall Be Despised."

(Prov.12:8) KJV

Proverbs of Solomon
Practical Instructions for Successful Living

March 11

"It Is Better To Be A Nobody With A Servant Than To Be Self-Important But Have No Food."

(Prov.12:9) NLT

"He That Is Despised, And Hath A Servant, Is Better Than He That Honoureth Himself, And Lacketh Bread."

(Prov.12:9) KJV

Proverbs of Solomon
Practical Instructions for Successful Living

March 12

"The Godly Are Concerned For The Welfare Of Their Animals, But Even the Kindness Of The Wicked Is Cruel."

(Prov.12:10) NLT

"A Righteous Man Regardeth The Life Of His Beast: But The Tender Mercies Of The Wicked Is Cruel."

(Prov.12:10) KJV

Proverbs of Solomon
Practical Instructions for Successful Living

March 13

"Hard Work Means Prosperity; Only Fools Idle Away Their Time.'

(Prov.12:11) NLT

"He That Tilleth His Land Shall Be Satisfied With Bread: But He That Followeth Vain Persons Is Void Of Understanding."

(Prov.12:11) KJV

Proverbs of Solomon
Practical Instructions for Successful Living

March 14

"Thieves Are Jealous Of Each Other's Loot, While The Godly Bear Their Own Fruit."

(Prov.12:12) NLT

"The Wicked Desireth The Net Of Evil Men: But The Root Of The Righteous Yieldeth Fruit."

(Prov.12:12) KJV

Proverbs of Solomon
Practical Instructions for Successful Living

March 15

"The Wicked Are Trapped By Their Own Words, But The Godly Escape Such Trouble."

(Prov.12:13) NLT

"The Wicked Is Snared By The Transgression Of His Lips: But The Just Shall Come Out Of Trouble."

(Prov.12:13) KJV

Proverbs of Solomon
Practical Instructions for Successful Living

March 16

"People Can Get Many Good Things By The Words They Say; The Work Of Their Hands Also Gives Them Many Benefits."

(Prov.12:14) NLT

"A Man Shall Be Satisfied With Good By The Fruit Of His Mouth: And the Recompense Of A Man's Hands Shall Be Rendered Unto Him."

(Prov.12:14) KJV

Proverbs of Solomon
Practical Instructions for Successful Living

March 17

"Fools Think They Need No Advice, But The Wise Listen To Others."

(Prov.12:15) NLT

"The Way Of A Fool Is Right In His Own Eyes: But He That Hearkeneth Unto Counsel Is Wise."

(Prov.12:15) KJV

Proverbs of Solomon
Practical Instructions for Successful Living

March 18

"A Fool Is Quick-Tempered, But A Wise Person Stays Calm When Insulted."

(Prov.12:16) NLT

"A Fool's Wrath Is Presently Known: But A Prudent Man Covereth Shame."

(Prov.12:16) KJV

Proverbs of Solomon
Practical Instructions for Successful Living

March 19

"An Honest Witness Tells The Truth; A False Witness Tells The Lies."

(Prov.12:17) NLT

"He That Speaketh Truth Sheweth Forth Righteousness: But A False Witness Tells Lies."

(Prov.12:17) KJV

Proverbs of Solomon
Practical Instructions for Successful Living

March 20

"Some People Make Cutting Remarks, But The Words Of The Wise Bring Healing."

(Prov.12:18) NLT

"There Is That Speaketh Like The Piercings Of The Sword: But The Tongue Of The Wise Is Health."

(Prov.12:18) KJV

Proverbs of Solomon
Practical Instructions for Successful Living

March 21

"Truth Stands The Test Of Time; Lies Are Soon Exposed."

(Prov.12:19) NLT

"The Lip Of Truth Shall Be Established For Ever: But A Lying Tongue Is But For A Moment."

(Prov.12:19) KJV

Proverbs of Solomon
Practical Instructions for Successful Living

March 22

"Deceit Fills Hearts That Are Plotting Evil; Joy Fills Hearts That Are Planning Peace."

(Prov.12:20) NLT

"Deceit Is In The Heart Of Them That Imagine Evil: But To The Counsellers Of Peace Is Joy."

(Prov.12:20) KJV

Proverbs of Solomon
Practical Instructions for Successful Living

March 23

"No Real Harm Befalls The Godly, But The Wicked Have Their Fill Of Trouble."

(Prov.12:21) NLT

"There Shall No Evil Happen To The Just: But The Wicked Shall Be Filled With Mischief."

(Prov.12:21) KJV

Proverbs of Solomon
Practical Instructions for Successful Living

March 24

"The LORD Hates Those Who Don't Keep Their Word, But He Delights In Those Who Do."

(Prov.12:22) NLT

"Lying Lips Are Abomination To The LORD: But They That Deal Truly Are His Delight."

(Prov.12:22) KJV

Proverbs of Solomon
Practical Instructions for Successful Living

March 25

"Wise People Don't Make A Show Of Their Knowledge, But Fools Broadcast Their Folly."

(Prov.12:23) NLT

"A Prudent Man Concealteth Knowledge: But The Heart Of Fools Proclaimeth Foolishness."

(Prov.12:23) KJV

Proverbs of Solomon
Practical Instructions for Successful Living

March 26

"Work Hard And Become A Leader; Be Lazy And Become A Slave."

(Prov.12:24) NLT

"The Hand Of The Diligent Shall Bear Rule: But The Slothful Shall Be Under Tribute."

(Prov.12:24) KJV

Proverbs of Solomon
Practical Instructions for Successful Living

March 27

"Worry Weighs A Person Down; An Encouraging Word Cheers A Person Up."

(Prov.12:25) NLT

"Heaviness In The Heart Of Man Maketh It Stoop: But A Good Word Maketh It Glad."

(Prov.12:25) KJV

Proverbs of Solomon
Practical Instructions for Successful Living

March 28

"The Godly Give Good Advice To Their Friends; The Wicked Lead Them Astray."

(Prov.12:26) NLT

"The Righteous Is More Excellent Than His Neighbour: But The Way Of The Wicked Seduceth Them."

(Prov.12:26)

Proverbs of Solomon
Practical Instructions for Successful Living

March 29

"Lazy People Don't Even Cook The Game They Catch, But The Diligent Make Use Of Everything They Find."

(Prov.12:27) NLT

"The Slothful Man Roasteth Not That Which He Took In Hunting; But The Substance Of A Diligent Man Is Precious."

(Prov.12:27) KJV

Proverbs of Solomon
Practical Instructions for Successful Living

March 30

"The Way Of The Godly Leads To Life; Their Path Does Not Lead To Death."

(Prov.12:28) NLT

"In The Way Of Righteousness Is Life; And In The Pathway Thereof There Is No Death."

(Prov.12:28) KJV

Proverbs of Solomon
Practical Instructions for Successful Living

March 31

"A Wise Child Accepts A Parent's Discipline; A Young Mocker Refuses To Listen."

(Prov.13:1) NLT

"A Wise Son Heareth His Father's Instruction: But A Scorner Heareth Not Rebuke."

(Prov.13:1) KJV

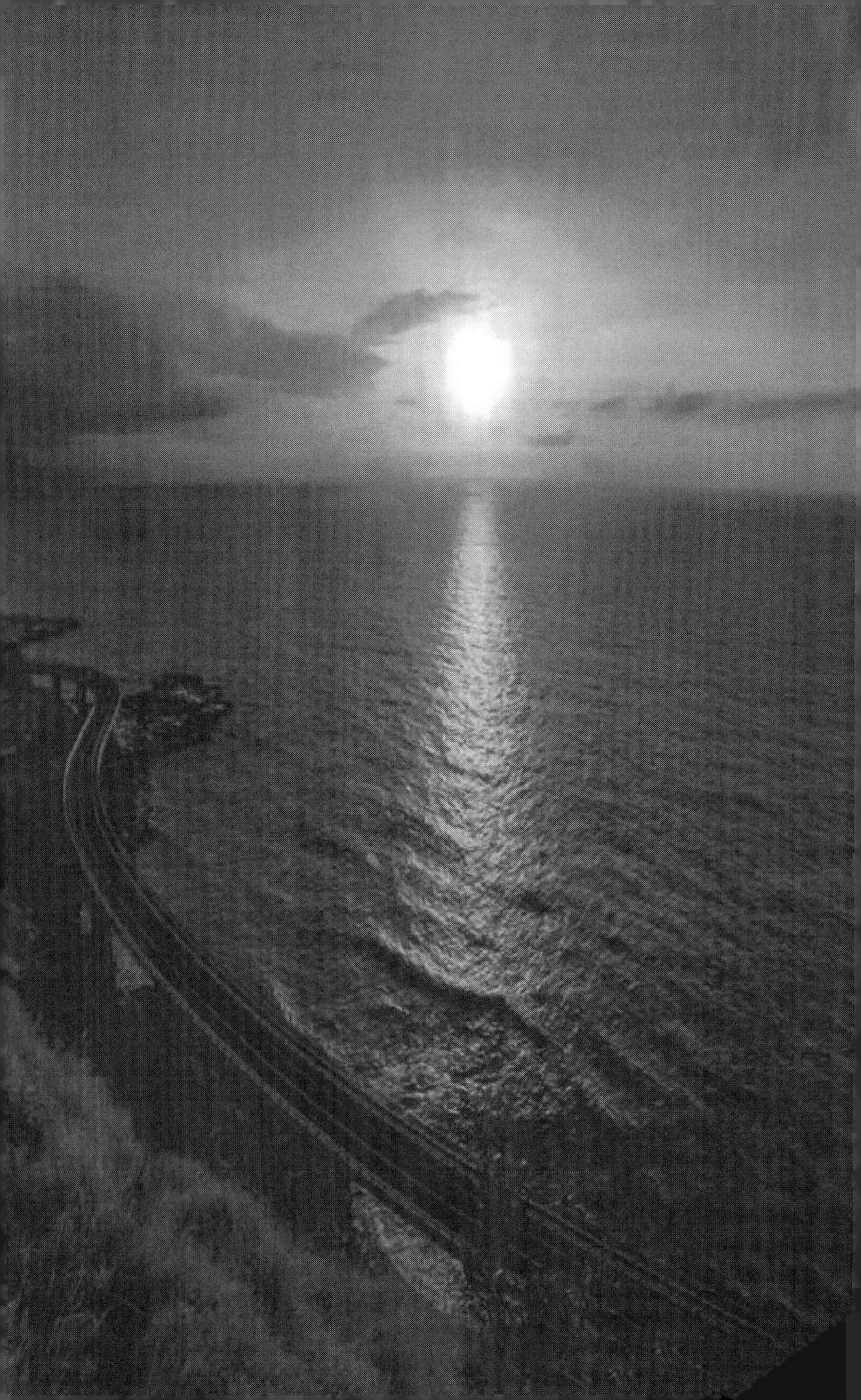

Proverbs of Solomon
Practical Instructions for Successful Living

April 1

"Good People Enjoy The Positive Results Of Their Words, But Those Who Are Treacherous Crave Violence."

(Prov.13:2) NLT

"A Man Shall Eat Good By The Fruit Of His Mouth: But The Soul Of The Transgressors Shall Eat Violence."

(Prov.13:2) KJV

Proverbs of Solomon
Practical Instructions for Successful Living

April 2

"Those Who Control Their Tongue Will Have A Long Life; A Quick Retort Can Ruin Everything."

(Prov.13:3) NLT

"He That Keepth His Mouth Keepeth His Life: But He That Openeth Wide His Lips Shall Have Destruction."

(Prov.13:3) KJV

Proverbs of Solomon
Practical Instructions for Successful Living

April 3

"Lazy People Want Much But Get Little, But Those Who Work Hard Will Prosper And Be Satisfied."

(Prov.13:4) NLT

"The Soul Of The Sluggard Desireth, And Hath Nothing: But The Soul Of The Diligent Shall Be Made Fat."

(Prov.13:4) KJV

Proverbs of Solomon
Practical Instructions for Successful Living

April 4

"Those Who Are Godly Hate Lies; The Wicked Come To Shame And Disgrace."

(Prov.13:5) NLT

"A Righteous Man Hateth Lying: But A Wicked Man Is Loathsome, And Cometh To Shame."

(Prov.13:5) KJV

Proverbs of Solomon
Practical Instructions for Successful Living

April 5

"Godliness Helps People All Through Life, While Evil Are Destroyed By Their Wickedness."

(Prov.13:6) NLT

"Righteousness Keepeth Him That Is Up-Right In The Way: But Wickedness Overthrowneth The Sinner."

(Prov.13:6) KJV

Proverbs of Solomon
Practical Instructions for Successful Living

April 6

"Some Who Are Poor Pretend To Be Rich; Others Who Are Rich Pretend To Be Poor."

(Prov.13:7) NLT

"There Is That Maketh Himself Rich, Yet Hath Nothing: There Is That Maketh Himself Poor, Yet Hath Great Riches."

(Prov.13:7) KJV

Proverbs of Solomon
Practical Instructions for Successful Living

April 7

"The Rich Can Pay Ransom, But The Poor Won't Even Get Threatened."

(Prov.13:8) NLT

"The Ransom Of A Man's Life Are His Riches: But The Poor Heareth Not Rebuke."

(Prov.13:8) KJV

Proverbs of Solomon
Practical Instructions for Successful Living

April 8

"The Life Of The Godly Is Full Of Light And Joy, But The Sinner's Light Is Snuffed Out."

(Prov.13:9) NLT

"The Light Of The Righteous Rejoiceth: But The Lamp Of The Wicked Shall Be Put Out."

(Prov.13:9) KJV

Proverbs of Solomon
Practical Instructions for Successful Living

April 9

"Pride Leads To Arguments; Those Who Take Advice Are Wise."

(Prov.13:10) NLT

"Only By Pride Cometh Contention: But With The Well Advised Is Wisdom."

(Prov.13:10) KJV

Proverbs of Solomon
Practical Instructions for Successful Living

April 10

"Wealth From Get-Rich-Quick Schemes quickly Disappear; Wealth From Hard Work Grows."

(Prov.13:11) NLT

"Wealth Gotten By Vanity Shall Be Diminished: But He That Gathereth By Labour Shall Increase."

(Prov.13:11) KJV

Proverbs of Solomon
Practical Instructions for Successful Living

April 11

"Hope Deferred Makes The Heart Sick, But When Dreams Come True, There Is Life And Joy."

(Prov.13:12) NLT

"Hope Deferred Maketh The Heart Sick: But When The Desire cometh, It Is A Tree Of Life."

(Prov.13:12) KJV

Proverbs of Solomon
Practical Instructions for Successful Living

April 12

"People Who Despise Advice Will Find Themselves In Trouble; Those Who Respect It Will Succeed."

(Prov.13:13) NLT

"Whoso Despiseth The Word Shall Be Destroyed: But He That Feareth The Commandment Shall Be Rewarded."

(Prov.13:13) KJV

Proverbs of Solomon
Practical Instructions for Successful Living

April 13

"The Advice Of The Wise Is Like A Life-Giving Fountain; Those Who Accept It Avoid The Snares Of Death."

(Prov.13:14) NLT

"The Law Of The Wise Is A Fountain Of Life, To Depart From The Snares Of Death."

(Prov.13:14) KJV

Proverbs of Solomon
Practical Instructions for Successful Living

April 14

"A Person With Good Sense Is Respected; A Treacherous Person Walks a Rocky Road."

(Prov.13:15) NLT

"Good Understanding Giveth Favour: But The Way Of Transgressors Is Hard."

(Prov.13:15) KJV

Proverbs of Solomon
Practical Instructions for Successful Living

April 15

"Wise People Think Before They Act; Fools Don't And Even Brag About It!"

(Prov.13:16) NLT

"Every Prudent Man Dealeth With Knowledge: But A Fool Layeth Open His Folly."

(Prov.13:16) KJV

Proverbs of Solomon
Practical Instructions for Successful Living

April 16

"An Unreliable Messenger Stumbles Into Trouble, But A Reliable Messenger Brings Healing."

(Prov.13:17) NLT

"A Wicked Messenger Falleth Into Mischief: But A Faithful Ambassador Is Health."

(Prov.13:17) KJV

Proverbs of Solomon
Practical Instructions for Successful Living

April 17

"If You Ignore Criticism, You Will End In Poverty And Disgrace; If You Accept Criticism, You Will Be Honored."

(Prov.13:18) NLT

"Poverty And Shame Shall Be To Him That Refuseth Instruction: But He That Regardeth Reproof Shall Be Honoured."

(Prov.13:18) KJV

Proverbs of Solomon
Practical Instructions for Successful Living

April 18

"It Is Pleasant To See Dreams Comes True, But Fools Will Not Turn From Evil To Attain Them."

(Prov.13:19) NLT

"The Desire Accomplished Is Sweet To The Soul: But It Is Abomination To Fools To Depart From Evil."

(Prov.13:19) KJV

Proverbs of Solomon
Practical Instructions for Successful Living

April 19

"Whoever Walks With The Wise Will Become Wise; Whoever Walks With Fools Will Suffer Harm."

(Prov.13:20) NLT

"He That Walketh With Wise Men Shall Be Wise: But A Companion of Fools Shall Be Destroyed."

(Prov.13:20) KJV

Proverbs of Solomon
Practical Instructions for Successful Living

April 20

"Trouble Chases Sinners, While Blessings Chase The Righteous!"

(Prov.13:21) NLT

"Evil Pursueth Sinners: But To The Righteous Good Shall Be Repaid."

(Prov.13:21) KJV

Proverbs of Solomon
Practical Instructions for Successful Living

April 21

"Good People Leave An Inheritance To Their Grandchildren, But The Sinner's Wealth Passes To The Godly."

(Prov.13:22) NLT

"A Good Man Leaveth An Inheritance To His Children's Children: And The Wealth Of The Sinner Is Laid Up For The Just."

(Prov.13:22) KJV

Proverbs of Solomon
Practical Instructions for Successful Living

April 22

"A Poor Person's Farm May Produce Much Food, But Injustice Sweeps It All Away."

(Prov.13:23) NLT

"Much Food Is In The Tillage Of The Poor: But There Is That Is Destroyed For Want Of Judgment."

(Prov.13:23) KJV

Proverbs of Solomon
Practical Instructions for Successful Living

April 23

"If You Refuse To Discipline Your Children, It Proves You Don't Love Them; If You Love Your Children, You Will Be Prompt To Discipline Them."

(Prov.12:24) NLT

"He That Spareth His Rod Hateth His Son: But He That Loveth Him Chasteneth Him Betimes."

(Prov.13:24) KJV

Proverbs of Solomon
Practical Instructions for Successful Living

April 24

"The Godly Eat To Their Heart's Content, But The Belly Of The Wicked Goes Hungry."

(Prov.13:25) NLT

"The Righteous Eateth To The Satisfying Of His Soul: But The Belly Of The Wicked Shall Want."

(Prov.13:25) KJV

Proverbs of Solomon
Practical Instructions for Successful Living

April 25

"A Wise Woman Builds Her House; A Foolish Woman Tears Hers Down With Her Own Hands."

(Prov.14:1) NLT

"Every Wise Woman Buildeth Her House: But The Foolish Plucketh It Down With Her Hands."

(Prov.14:1) KJV

Proverbs of Solomon
Practical Instructions for Successful Living

April 26

"Those Who Follow The Right Path Fear The LORD; Those Who Take The Wrong Path Despise Him."

(Prov.14:2) NLT

"He That Walketh In His Uprightness Feareth The LORD: But He That Is Perverse In His Ways Despiseth Him."

(Prov.14:2) KJV

Proverbs of Solomon
Practical Instructions for Successful Living

April 27

"A Fool's Proud Talk Becomes A Rod That Beats Him, But The Words Of The Wise Keep Them Safe."

(Prov.14:3) NLT

"In the Mouth Of The Foolish Is A Rod Of Pride: But The Lips Of The Wise Shall Preserve Them."

(Prov.14:3) KJV

Proverbs of Solomon
Practical Instructions for Successful Living

April 28

"An Empty Stable Stays Clean, But No Income comes From An Empty Stable."

(Prov.14:4) NLT

"Where No Oxen Are, The Crib Is Clean: But Much Increase Is By The Strength Of The Ox."

(Prov.14:4)

Proverbs of Solomon
Practical Instructions for Successful Living

April 29

"A Truthful Witness Does Not Lie; A False Witness Breathes Lies."

(Prov.14:5) NLT

"A Faithful Witness Will Not Lie: But A False Witness Will Utter Lies."

(Prov.14:5) KJV

Proverbs of Solomon
Practical Instructions for Successful Living

April 30

"A Mocker Seeks Wisdom And Never Finds It, But Knowledge Comes Easily To Those With Understanding."

(Prov.14:6) NLT

"A Scorner Seeketh Wisdom, And Findeth It not: But Knowledge Is Easy Unto Him That Understandeth."

(Prov.14:6) KJV

Proverbs of Solomon
Practical Instructions for Successful Living

May 1

"Stay Away From Fools, For You Won't Find Knowledge There."

(Prov.14:7) NLT

"Go From The Presence Of A Foolish Man, When Thou Perceivest Not In Him The Lips Of Knowledge."

(Prov.14:7) KJV

Proverbs of Solomon
Practical Instructions for Successful Living

May 2

"The Wise Look Ahead To See What Is Coming, But Fools Deceive Themselves."

(Prov.14:8) NLT

"The Wisdom Of The Prudent Is To Understand His Way: But The Folly Of Fools Is Deceit."

(Prov.14:8) KJV

Proverbs of Solomon
Practical Instructions for Successful Living

May 3

"Fools Make Fun Of Guilt, But The Godly Acknowledge It And Seek Reconciliation."

(Prov.14:9) NLT

"Fools Make A Mock Of Sin: But Among The Righteous There Is Favour."

(Prov.14:9) KJV

Proverbs of Solomon
Practical Instructions for Successful Living

May 4

"Each Heart Knows Its Own Bitterness, And No One Else Can Fully Share Its Joy."

(Prov.14:10) NLT

"The Heart Knoweth His Own Bitterness; And A Stranger Doth Not Intermeddle With His Joy."

(Prov.14:10) KJV

Proverbs of Solomon
Practical Instructions for Successful Living

May 5

"The House Of The Wicked Will Perish, But The Tent Of The Godly Will Flourish."

(Prov.14:11) NLT

"The House Of The Wicked Shall Be Overthrown: But The Tabernacle Of The Upright Shall Flourish."

(Prov.14:11) KJV

Proverbs of Solomon
Practical Instructions for Successful Living

May 6

"There Is A Path Before Each Person That Seems Right, But It Ends In Death."

(Prov.14:12) NLT

"There Is A Way Which Seemeth Right Unto A Man, But The End Thereof Are the Ways Of Death."

(Prov.14:12) KJV

Proverbs of Solomon
Practical Instructions for Successful Living

May 7

"Laughter Can Conceal A Heavy Heart; When The Laughter Ends, The Grief Remains."

(Prov.14:13) NLT

"Even In Laughter The Heart Is Sorrowful: And The End Of That Mirth Is Heaviness."

(Prov.14:13) KJV

Proverbs of Solomon
Practical Instructions for Successful Living

May 8

"Backsliders Get What They Deserve; Good People Receive Their Reward."

(Prov.14:14) NLT

"The Backslider In Heart Shall Be Filled With His Own Ways: And A Good Man Shall Be Satisfied From Himself."

(Prov.14:14) KJV

Proverbs of Solomon
Practical Instructions for Successful Living

May 9

"Only Simpletons Believe Everything They Are Told! The Prudent Carefully Consider Their Steps."

(Prov.14:15) NLT

"The Simple Believeth Every Word: But The Prudent Man Looketh Well To His Going."

(Prov.14:15) KJV

Proverbs of Solomon
Practical Instructions for Successful Living

May 10

"The Wise Are Cautious And Avoid Danger; Fools Plunge Ahead With Great Confidence."

(Prov.14:16) NLT

"A Wise Man Feareth, And Departeth From Evil: But The Fool Rageth, And Is Confident."

(Prov.14:16) KJV

Proverbs of Solomon
Practical Instructions for Successful Living

May 11

"Those Who Are Short-Tempered Do Foolish Things And Schemers Are Hated."

(Prov.14:17) NLT

"He That Is Soon Angry Dealeth Foolishly: And A Man Of Wicked Devices Is Hated."

(Prov.14:17) KJV

Proverbs of Solomon
Practical Instructions for Successful Living

May 12

"The Simpleton Is Clothed With Folly, But The Wise Person Is Crowned With Knowledge."

(Prov.14:18) NLT

"The Simple Inherit Folly: But The Prudent Are Crowned With Knowledge."

(Prov.14:18) KJV

Proverbs of Solomon
Practical Instructions for Successful Living

May 13

"Evil People Will Bow Before Good People; The Wicked Will Bow Before The Gates Of The Godly."

(Prov.14:19) NLT

"The Evil Will Bow Before The Good; And The Wicked At The Gates Of The Righteous."

(Prov.14:19) KJV

Proverbs of Solomon
Practical Instructions for Successful Living

May 14

"The Poor Are Despised Even By Their Neighbors, While The Rich Have Many "Friends."

(Prov14:20) NLT

"The Poor Is Hated Even Of His Own Neighbor: But The Rich Hath Many Friends."

(Prov.14:20) KJV

Proverbs of Solomon
Practical Instructions for Successful Living

May 15

"It Is Sin To Despise One's Neighbors; Blessed Are Those Who Help The Poor."

(Prov.14:21) NLT

"He That Despiseth His Neighbor Sinneth: But He That Hath Mercy On The Poor, Happy Is He."

(Prov.14:21) KJV

Proverbs of Solomon
Practical Instructions for Successful Living

May 16

"If You Plot Evil, You Will Be Lost; But If You Plan Good, You Will Be Granted Unfailing Love And Faithfulness."

(Prov.14:22) NLT

"Do They Not Err That Devise Evil? But Mercy And Truth Shall Be To Them That Devise Good."

(Prov.14:22) KJV

Proverbs of Solomon
Practical Instructions for Successful Living

May 17

"Work Brings Profit, But Mere Talk Leads To Poverty!"

(Prov.14:23) NLT

"In All Labour There Is Profit: But The Talk The Lips Tendeth Only To Penury."

(Prov.14:23) KJV

Proverbs of Solomon
Practical Instructions for Successful Living

May 18

"Wealth Is A Crown For The Wise; The Effort Of Fools Yields Only Folly."

(Prov.14:24) NLT

"The Crown Of The Wise Is Their Riches: But The Foolishness Of Fools Is Folly."

(Prov.14:24) KJV

Proverbs of Solomon
Practical Instructions for Successful Living

May 19

"A Truthful Witness Saves Lives, But A False Witness Is A Traitor."

(Prov.14:25) NLT

"A True Witness Delivereth Souls: But A Deceitful Witness Speaketh Lies."

(Prov.14:25) KJV

Proverbs of Solomon
Practical Instructions for Successful Living

May 20

"Those Who Fear The LORD Are Secure; He Will Be A Place Of Refuge For Their Children."

(Prov.14:26) NLT

"In The Fear Of The LORD Is Strong Confidence: And His Children Shall Have A Place Of Refuge."

(Prov.14:26) KJV

Proverbs of Solomon
Practical Instructions for Successful Living

May 21

"Fear Of The LORD Is A Life-Giving Fountain; It Offers Escape From The Snares Of Death."

(Prov.14:27) NLT

"The Fear Of The LORD is A Fountain Of Life, To Depart From The Snares Of Death."

(Prov.14:27) KJV

Proverbs of Solomon
Practical Instructions for Successful Living

May 22

"A Growing Population Is A King's Glory; A Dwindling Nation Is His Doom."

(Prov.14:28) NLT

"In The Multitude Of People Is The King's Honour: But In The Want Of People Is The Destruction Of The Prince."

(Prov.14:28) KJV

Proverbs of Solomon
Practical Instructions for Successful Living

May 23

"Those Who Control Their Anger Have Great Understanding; Those With a Hasty Temper Will Make Mistakes."

(Prov.14:29) NLT

"He That Is Slow In Wrath Is Of Great Understanding: But He That Is Hasty Of Spirit Exalteth Folly."

(Prov.14:29) KJV

Proverbs of Solomon
Practical Instructions for Successful Living

May 24

"A Relaxed Attitude Lengthens Life; Jealousy Rots It Away."

(Prov.14:30) NLT

"A Sound Heart Is The Life Of The Flesh: But Envy The Rottenness Of The Bones."

(Prov.14:30) KJV

Proverbs of Solomon
Practical Instructions for Successful Living

May 25

"Those Who Oppress The Poor Insult Their Maker, But Those Who Help The Poor Honor Him."

(Prov.14:31) NLT

"He That Oppressed The Poor Reproacheth His Maker: But He That Honoureth Him Hath Mercy On The Poor."

(Prov.14:31) KJV

Proverbs of Solomon
Practical Instructions for Successful Living

May 26

"The Wicked Are Crushed By Their Sins, But The Godly Have Refuge When They Die."

(Prov.14:32) NLT

"The Wicked Is Driven Away In His Wickedness: But The Righteous Hath Hope In His Death."

(Prov.14:32) KJV

Proverbs of Solomon
Practical Instructions for Successful Living

May 27

"Wisdom Is enshrined In An Understanding Heart; Wisdom Is Not Found Among Fools."

(Prov.14:33) NLT

"Wisdom Resteth In The Heart Of Him That Hath Understanding: But That Which Is In The Midst Of Fools Is Made Known."

(Prov.14:33) KJV

Proverbs of Solomon
Practical Instructions for Successful Living

May 28

"Godliness Exalts A Nation, But Sin Is A Disgrace To Any People."

(Prov.14:34) NLT

"Righteousness Exalteth A Nation: But Sin Is A Reproach To Any People."

(Prov.14:34) KJV

Proverbs of Solomon
Practical Instructions for Successful Living

May 29

"A King Rejoices In Servants Who Know What They Are Doing; He Is Angry With Those Who Cause Trouble."

(Prov.14:35) NLT

"The King's Favour Is Toward A Wise Servant: But His Wrath Is Against Him that Causeth Shame."

(Prov.14:35) KJV

Proverbs of Solomon
Practical Instructions for Successful Living

May 30

"A Gentle Answer Turns Away Wrath, But Harsh Words Stir Up Anger."

(Prov.15:1) NLT

"A Soft Answers Turneth Away Wrath: But Grievous Words Stir Up Anger."

(Prov.15:1) KJV

Proverbs of Solomon
Practical Instructions for Successful Living

May 31

"The Wise Person Makes Learning A Joy; Fools Spout Only Foolishness."

(Prov.15:2) NLT

"The Tongue Of The Wise Useth Knowledge Aright: But The Mouth Of Fools Poureth Out Foolishness."

(Prov.15:2) KJV

Proverbs of Solomon
Practical Instructions for Successful Living

June 1

"The LORD Is Watching Everywhere, Keeping His Eye On Both The Evil And The Good."

(Prov.15:3) NLT

"The Eyes Of The LORD Are In Every Place, Beholding The Evil And The Good."

(Prov.15:3) KJV

Proverbs of Solomon
Practical Instructions for Successful Living

June 2

"Gentle Words Bring Life And Health; A Deceitful Tongue Crushes The Spirit."

(Prov.15:4) NLT

"A Wholesome Tongue Is A Tree Of Life: But Perverseness Therein Is A Breach In The Spirit."

(Prov.15:4) KJV

Proverbs of Solomon
Practical Instructions for Successful Living

June 3

"Only A Fool Despises A Parent's Discipline; Whoever Learns From Correction Is Wise."

(Prov.15:5) NLT

"A Fool Despises His Father's Instructions: But He That Regardeth Reproof Is Prudent."

(Prov.15:5) KJV

Proverbs of Solomon
Practical Instructions for Successful Living

June 4

"There Is Treasure In The House Of The Godly, But The Earnings Of The Wicked Bring Trouble."

(Prov.15:6) NLT

"In the House Of The Righteous Is Much Treasure: But In The Revenues Of The Wicked Is Trouble."

(Prov.15:6) KJV

Proverbs of Solomon
Practical Instructions for Successful Living

June 5

"Only The Wise Can Give Good Advice; Fools Cannot Do So."

(Prov.15:7) NLT

"The Lips Of The Wise Disperse Knowledge: But The Heart Of The Foolish Doeth Not So."

(Prov.15:7) KJV

Proverbs of Solomon
Practical Instructions for Successful Living

June 6

"The LORD Hates The Sacrifice Of The Wicked, But He Delights In The Prayers Of The Upright."

(Prov.15:8) NLT

"The Sacrifice Of The Wicked Is An Abomination To The LORD: But The Prayer Of The Upright Is His Delight."

(Prov15:8) KJV

Proverbs of Solomon
Practical Instructions for Successful Living

June 7

"The LORD Despised The Ways Of The Wicked, But He Loves Those Who Pursue Godliness."

(Prov.15:9) NLT

"The Way Of The Wicked Is An Abomination Unto The LORD: But He Loveth Him That Followeth After Righteousness."

(Prov.15:9) KJV

Proverbs of Solomon
Practical Instructions for Successful Living

June 8

"Whoever Abandons The Right Path Will Be Severely Punished: Whoever Hates Correction Will Die."

(Prov.15:10) NLT

"Corrections Is Grievous Unto Him That Forsaken The Way: And He That Hateth Reproof Shall Die."

(Prov.15:10) KJV

Proverbs of Solomon
Practical Instructions for Successful Living

June 9

"Even The Depths Of Death And Destruction Are Known By The LORD. How Much More Does He Know the Human Heart!"

(Prov.15:11) NLT

"Hell And Destruction Are Before The LORD: How Much More Then The Hearts Of The Children Of Men?"

(Prov.15:11) KJV

Proverbs of Solomon
Practical Instructions for Successful Living

June 10

"Mockers Don't Love Them Who Rebuke Them, So They Stay Away From The Wise."

(Prov.15:12) NLT

"A Scorner Loveth Not One That Reproveth Him: Neither Will He Go Unto The Wise."

(Prov.15:12) KJV

Proverbs of Solomon
Practical Instructions for Successful Living

June 11

"A Glad Heart Makes A Happy Face; A Broken Heart Crushes The Spirit."

(Prov.15:13) NLT

"A Merry Heart Maketh A Cheerful Countennance: But By Sorrow Of The Heart The Spirit Is Broken."

(Prov.15:13) KJV

Proverbs of Solomon
Practical Instructions for Successful Living

June 12

"A Wise Person Is Hungry For Truth, While The Fool Feeds On Trash."

(Prov.15:14) NLT

"The Heart Of Him That Hath Understanding Seeketh Knowledge: But The Mouth Of Fools Feedeth On Foolishness."

(Prov.15:14) KJV

Proverbs of Solomon
Practical Instructions for Successful Living

June 13

"For The Despondent, Every Day Brings Trouble; For The Happy Heart, Life Is A Continual Feast."

(Prov.15:15) NLT

"All The Days Of The Afflicted Are Evil: But He That Is Of A Merry Heart Hath A Continual Feast."

(Prov.15:15) KJV

Proverbs of Solomon
Practical Instructions for Successful Living

June 14

"It Is Better To Have Little With Fear Of The LORD Than to Have Great Treasure With Turmoil."

(Prov.15:16) NLT

"Better Is Little With The Fear Of The LORD Than Great Treasure And Trouble Therewith."

(Prov.15:16) KJV

Proverbs of Solomon
Practical Instructions for Successful Living

June 15

"A Bowl Of Soup With Someone You Love Is Better Than Steak With Someone You Hate."

(Prov.15:17) NLT

"Better Is A Dinner Of Herbs Where Love Is, Than A Stalled Ox And Hatred Therewith."

(Prov.15:17) KJV

Proverbs of Solomon
Practical Instructions for Successful Living

June 16

"A Hothead Starts Fights; A Cool-Tempered Person Tries To Stop Them."

(Prov.15:18) NLT

"A Wrathful Man Stirreth Up Strife: But He That Is Slow To Anger Appeaseth Strife."

(Prov.15:18) KJV

Proverbs of Solomon
Practical Instructions for Successful Living

June 17

"A Lazy Person Has Trouble All Through Life; The Path Of The Upright Is Easy!"

(Prov.15:19) NLT

"The Way Of A Slothful Man Is As An Hedge Of Thorns: But The Way Of The Righteous Is Made Plain."

(Prov.15:19) KJV

Proverbs of Solomon
Practical Instructions for Successful Living

June 18

"Sensible Children Bring Joy To Their Father; Foolish Children Despise Their Mother."

(Prov.15:20) NLT

"A Wise Son Maketh A Glad Father: But A Foolish Man Despiseth His Mother."

(Prov.15:20) KJV

Proverbs of Solomon
Practical Instructions for Successful Living

June 19

"Foolishness Brings Joy To Those Who Have No Sense; A Sensible Person Stays On The Right Path."

(Prov.15:21) NLT

"Folly Is Joy To Him That Is Destitute Of Wisdom: But A Man Of Understanding Walketh Uprightly."

(Prov.15:21) KJV

Proverbs of Solomon
Practical Instructions for Successful Living

June 20

"Plans Go Wrong For Lack Of Advice; May Counselors Bring Success."

(Prov.15:22) NLT

"Without Counsel Purposes Are Disappointed: But In The Multitude Of The Counsellors They Are Established."

(Prov.15:22) KJV

Proverbs of Solomon
Practical Instructions for Successful Living

June 21

"Everyone Enjoys a Fitting Reply; It Is Wonderful To Say The Right Thing At The Right Time!"

(Prov.15:23) NLT

"A Man Hath Joy By The Answer Of His Mouth: And A Word Spoken In Due Season, How Good Is It!"

(Prov.15:23) KJV

Proverbs of Solomon
Practical Instructions for Successful Living

June 22

"The Path Of The Wise Leads To Life Above; They Leave The Grave Behind."

(Prov.15:24) NLT

"The Way Of Life Is Above To The Wise, That He May Depart From Hell Beneath."

(Prov.15:24) KJV

Proverbs of Solomon
Practical Instructions for Successful Living

June 23

"The LORD Destroys The House Of The Proud, But He Protects The Property Of Widows."

(Prov.15:25) NLT

"The LORD Will Destroy The House Of The Proud: But He Will Establish The Border Of The Widow."

(Prov.15:25) KJV

Proverbs of Solomon
Practical Instructions for Successful Living

June 24

"The LORD Despises The Thoughts Of The Wicked, But He Delights In Pure Words."

(Prov.15:26) NLT

"The Thoughts Of The Wicked Are An Abomination To The LORD: But The Words Of The Pure Are Pleasant Words."

(Prov.15:26) KJV

Proverbs of Solomon
Practical Instructions for Successful Living

June 25

"Dishonest Money Brings Grief To The Whole Family, But Those Who Hate Bribes Will Live."

(Prov.15:27) NLT

"He That Is Greedy Of Gain Troubleth His Own House; But He That Hateth Gifts Shall Live."

(Prov.15:27) KJV

Proverbs of Solomon
Practical Instructions for Successful Living

June 26

"The Godly Think Before Speaking; The Wicked Spout Evil Words."

(Prov.15:28) NLT

"The Heart Of The Righteous Studieth To Answer: But The Mouth Of The Wicked Poureth Out Evil Things."

(Prov.15:28) KJV

Proverbs of Solomon
Practical Instructions for Successful Living

June 27

"The LORD Is Far From The Wicked, But He Hears The Prayers Of The Righteous."

(Prov.15:29) NLT

"The LORD Is Far From The Wicked: But He Heareth The Prayer Of The Righteous."

(Prov.15:29) KJV

Proverbs of Solomon
Practical Instructions for Successful Living

June 28

"A Cheerful Look Brings Joy To The Heart; Good News Makes For Good Health."

(Prov.15:30) NLT

"The Light Of The Eyes Rejoiceth The Heart: And A Good Report Maketh The Bones Fat."

(Prov.15:30) KJV

Proverbs of Solomon
Practical Instructions for Successful Living

June 29

"If You Listen To Constructive Criticism, You Will Be At Home Among The Wise."

(Prov.15:31) NLT

"The Ear That Heareth The Reproof Of Life Abideth Among The Wise."

(Prov.15:31) KJV

Proverbs of Solomon
Practical Instructions for Successful Living

June 30

"If You Reject Criticism, You Only Harm Yourself; But If You Listen to Correction, You Grow In Understanding."

(Prov.15:32) NLT

"He That Refuseth Instruction Despiseth His Own Soul: But He That Heareth Reproof Getteth Understanding."

(Prov.15:32) KJV

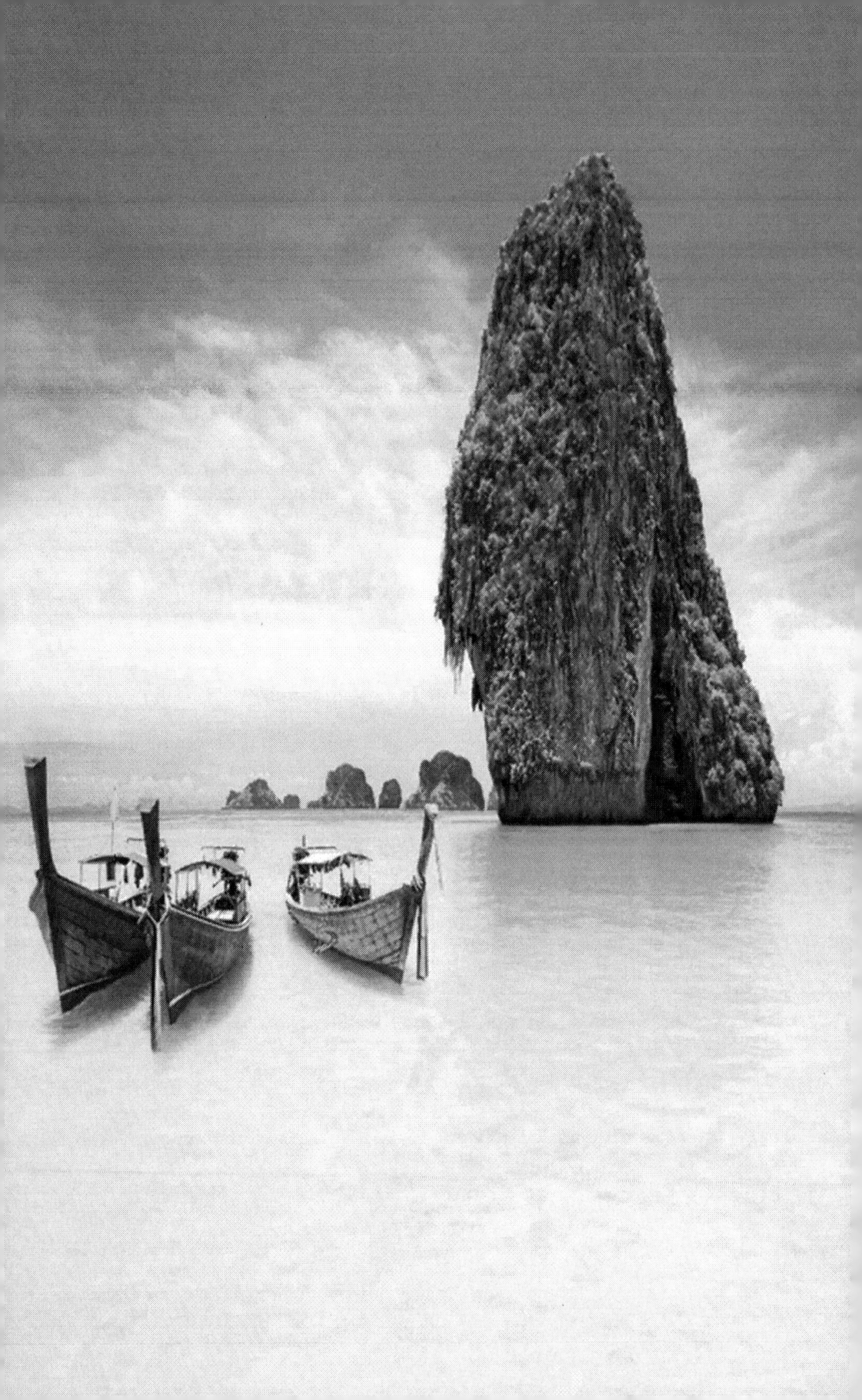

Proverbs of Solomon
Practical Instructions for Successful Living

July 1

"Fear Of The LORD Teaches A Person to Be Wise; Humility Precedes Honor."

(Prov.15:33) NLT

"The Fear Of The LORD Is The Instruction Of Wisdom; And Before Honour Is Humility."

(Prov.15:33) KJV

Proverbs of Solomon
Practical Instructions for Successful Living

July 2

"We Can Gather Our Thoughts, But The LORD Gives The Right Answer."

(Prov.16:1) NLT

"The Preparations Of The Heart In Man, And The Answer Of The Tongue, Is From The LORD."

(Prov.16:1) KJV

Proverbs of Solomon
Practical Instructions for Successful Living

July 3

"People May Be Pure In Their Own Eyes, But The LORD Examines Their Motives."

(Prov.16:2) NLT

"All The Ways Of Man Are Clean In His Own Eyes; But The LORD Weigheth The Spirits."

(Prov.16:2) KJV

Proverbs of Solomon
Practical Instructions for Successful Living

July 4

"Commit Your Work To The LORD, And Then Your Plans Will Succeed."

(Prov.16:3) NLT

"Commit Thy Works Unto the LORD, And Thy Thoughts Shall Be Established."

(Prov.16:3) KJV

Proverbs of Solomon
Practical Instructions for Successful Living

July 5

"The LORD Has Made Everything For His Own Purposes, Even The Wicked For Punishment."

(Prov.16:4) NLT

"The LORD Hath Made All Things For Himself: Yea, Even The Wicked For The Day Of Evil."

(Prov.16:4) KJV

Proverbs of Solomon
Practical Instructions for Successful Living

July 6

"The LORD Despises Pride; Be Assured That The Proud Will Be Punished."

(Prov.16:5) NLT

"Every One That Is Proud In Heart Is An Abomination To The LORD: Though Hand Join In Hand, He Shall Be Unpunished."

(Prov.16:5) KJV

Proverbs of Solomon
Practical Instructions for Successful Living

July 7

"Unfailing Love And Faithfulness Cover Sin; Evil Is Avoided By Fear Of The LORD."

(Prov.16:6) NLT

"By Mercy And Truth Iniquity Is Purged: And By The Fear Of The LORD Men Depart From Evil."

(Prov.16:6) KJV

Proverbs of Solomon
Practical Instructions for Successful Living

July 8

"When The Ways Of The People Please The LORD, He Make Even Their Enemies Live At Peace With Them."

(Prov.16:7) NLT

"When A Man's Ways Please The LORD, He Maketh Even His Enemies To Be At Peace With Him."

(Prov.16:7) KJV

Proverbs of Solomon
Practical Instructions for Successful Living

July 9

"It Is Better To Be Poor And Godly Than Rich And Dishonest."

(Prov.16:8) NLT

"Better Is A Little With Righteousness Than Great Revenues Without Right."

(Prov.16:8) KJV

Proverbs of Solomon
Practical Instructions for Successful Living

July 10

"We Can Make Our Plans, But The LORD Determines Our Steps."

(Prov.16:9) NLT

"A Man's Heart Deviseth His Way: But The LORD Directeth His Steps."

(Prov.16:9) KJV

Proverbs of Solomon
Practical Instructions for Successful Living

July 11

"The King Speaks With Divine Wisdom; He Must Never Judge Unfairly."

(Prov.16:10) NLT

"A Divine Sentence Is In The Lips Of The King; His Mouth Transgresseth Not In Judgement."

(Prov.16:10) KJV

Proverbs of Solomon
Practical Instructions for Successful Living

July 12

"The LORD Demands Fairness In Every Business Deal; He Sets The Standard."

(Prov.16:11) NLT

"A Just Weight And Balance Are The LORD's: All The Weights Of The Bag Are His Work."

(Prov.16:11) KJV

Proverbs of Solomon
Practical Instructions for Successful Living

July 13

"A King Despises Wrong Doing, For His Rule Depends On His Justice."

(Prov.16:12) NLT

"It Is An Abomination To Kings To Commit Wickedness: For The Throne Is Established By Righteousness."

(Prov.16:12) KJV

Proverbs of Solomon
Practical Instructions for Successful Living

July 14

"The King Is Pleased With Righteous Lips; He Loves Those Who Speak Honestly."

(Prov.16:13) NLT

"Righteous Lips Are The Delight Of Kings; And They Love Him That Speaketh Right."

(Prov.16:13) KJV

Proverbs of Solomon
Practical Instructions for Successful Living

July 15

"The Anger Of The King Is a Deadly Threat; The Wise Do What They Can Do To Appease It."

(Prov.16:14) NLT

"The Wrath Of A King Is As Messengers Of Death: But A Wise Man Will Pacify It."

(Prov.16:14) KJV

Proverbs of Solomon
Practical Instructions for Successful Living

July 16

"When The King Smiles, There Is Life; His Favor Refreshes Like A Gentle Rain."

(Prov.16:15) NLT

"In The Light Of The King's Countenance Is Life; And His Favour Is As A Cloud Of The Latter Rain."

(Prov.16:15) KJV

Proverbs of Solomon
Practical Instructions for Successful Living

July 17

"How Much Better To Get Wisdom Than Gold, And Understanding Than Silver!"

(Prov.16:16) NLT

"How Much Better Is It To Get Wisdom Than Gold! And To Get Understanding Rather To Be Chosen Than Silver!"

(Prov.16:16) KJV

Proverbs of Solomon
Practical Instructions for Successful Living

July 18

"The Path Of The Upright Leads Away From Evil; Whoever Follows That Path Is Safe."

(Prov.16:17) NLT

"The Highway Of The Upright Is To Depart From Evil: He That Keepeth His Way Preserveth His Soul."

(Prov.16:17) KJV

Proverbs of Solomon
Practical Instructions for Successful Living

July 19

"Pride Goes Before Destruction, And Haughtiness Before A Fall."

(Prov.16:18) NLT

"Pride Goeth Before Destruction, And An Haughty Spirit Before A Fall."

(Prov.16:18) KJV

Proverbs of Solomon
Practical Instructions for Successful Living

July 20

"It Is Better To Live Humbly With The Poor Than To Share Plunder With The Proud."

(Prov.16:19) NLT

"Better It Is To Be Of A Humble Spirit With The Lowly, Than To Divide The Spoil With The Proud."

(Prov.16:19) KJV

Proverbs of Solomon
Practical Instructions for Successful Living

July 21

"Those Who Listen To Instruction Will Prosper; Those Who Trust The LORD Will Be Happy."

(Prov.16:20) NLT

"He That Handleth A Matter Wisely Shall Find Good: And Whoso Trusteth In The LORD, Happy Is He."

(Prov.16:20) KJV

Proverbs of Solomon
Practical Instructions for Successful Living

July 22

"The Wise Are Known For Their Understanding, And Instruction Is Appreciated If It's Well Presented."

(Prov.16:21) NLT

"The Wise In Heart Shall Be Called Prudent: And The Sweetness Of The Lips Increaseth Learning."

(Prov.16:21) KJV

Proverbs of Solomon
Practical Instructions for Successful Living

July 23

"Discretion Is A Life-Giving Fountain To Those Who Possess It, But Discipline Is Wasted On Fools."

(Prov.16:22) NLT

"Understanding Is A Wellspring Of Life Unto That Hath It: But The Instruction Of Fools Is Folly."

(Prov.16:22) KJV

Proverbs of Solomon
Practical Instructions for Successful Living

July 24

"From A Wise Mind Comes Wise Speech; The Words Of The Wise Are Persuasive."

(Prov.16:23) NLT

"The Heart Of The Wise Teacheth His Mouth, And Addeth Learning To His Lips."

(Prov.16:23) KJV

Proverbs of Solomon
Practical Instructions for Successful Living

July 25

"Kind Words Are Like Honey-Sweet To The Soul And Healthy For The Body."

(Prov.16:24) NLT

"Pleasant Words Are As A Honeycomb, Sweet To The Soul, And Health To The Bones."

(Prov.16:24) KJV

Proverbs of Solomon
Practical Instructions for Successful Living

July 26

"There Is A Path Before Each Person That Seems Right, But It Ends In Death."

(Prov.16:25) NLT

"There Is A Way That Seemeth Right Unto A Man, But The End Thereof Are The Ways Of Death."

(Prov.16:25) KJV

Proverbs of Solomon
Practical Instructions for Successful Living

July 27

"It Is Good For Workers To Have An Appetite; An Empty Stomach Drives Them On."

(Prov.16:26) NLT

"He That Laboureth Laboureth For Himself; For His Mouth Craveth It Of Him."

(Prov.16:26) KJV

Proverbs of Solomon
Practical Instructions for Successful Living

July 28

"Scoundrels Hunt For Scandal; Their Words Are A Destructive Blaze."

(Prov.16:27) NLT

"An Ungodly Man Diggeth Up Evil: And In His Lips There Is As A Burning Fire."

(Prov.16:27) KJV

Proverbs of Solomon
Practical Instructions for Successful Living

July 29

"A Troublemaker Plants Seeds Of Strife; Gossip Separates The Best Of Friends."

(Prov.16:28) NLT

"A Froward Man Soweth Strife: And A Whisperer Separateth Chief Friends."

(Prov.16:28) KJV

Proverbs of Solomon
Practical Instructions for Successful Living

July 30

"Violent People Deceive Their Companions, Leading Them Down A Harmful Path."

(Prov.16:29) NLT

"A Violent Man Enticeth His Neighbour, And Leadeth Him Into The Way That Is Not Good."

(Prov.16:29) KJV

Proverbs of Solomon
Practical Instructions for Successful Living

July 31

"With Narrowed Eyes, They Plot Evil; With Out A Word, They Plan Their Mischief."

(Prov.16:30) NLT

"He Shutteth His Eyes To Devise Froward Things: Moving His Lips He Bringeth Evil To Pass."

(Prov.16:30) KJV

Proverbs of Solomon
Practical Instructions for Successful Living

August 1

"Gray Hair Is A Crown Of Glory; It Is Gained By Living A Godly Life."

(Prov.16:31) NLT

"The Hoary Head Is A Crown Of Glory, If It Be Found In The Way Of Righteousness."

(Prov.16:31) KJV

Proverbs of Solomon
Practical Instructions for Successful Living

August 2

"It Is Better To Be Patient Than Powerful; It Is Better To Have Self-Control Than To Conquer A City."

(Prov.16:32) NLT

"He That Is Slow To Anger Is Better Than The Mighty; And He That Ruleth His Spirit Than He That Taketh A City."

(Prov.16:32) KJV

Proverbs of Solomon
Practical Instructions for Successful Living

August 3

"We May Throw The Dice, But The LORD Determines How They Fall."

(Prov.16:33) NLT

"The Lot Is Cast Into The Lap; But The Whole Disposing Thereof Is Of The LORD."

(Prov.16:33) KJV

Proverbs of Solomon
Practical Instructions for Successful Living

August 4

"A Dry Crust Eaten In Peace Is Better Than A Great Feast With Strife."

(Prov.17:1) NLT

"Better Is Dry Morsel, And Quietness Therewith, Than A House Full Of Sacrifices With Strife."

(Prov.17:1) KJV

Proverbs of Solomon
Practical Instructions for Successful Living

August 5

"A Wise Slave Will Rule Over The Master's Shameful Sons And Will Share Their Inheritance."

(Prov.17:2) NLT

"A Wise Servant Shall Have Rule Over A Son That Causeth Shame, And Shall Have Part Of The Inheritance Among The Brethren."

(Prov.17:2) KJV

Proverbs of Solomon
Practical Instructions for Successful Living

August 6

"Fire Tests The Purity Of Silver And Gold, But The LORD Tests The Heart."

(Prov.17:3) NLT

"The Fining Pot Is For Silver, And The Furnace For Gold: But The LORD Trieth The Hearts."

(Prov.17:3) KJV

Proverbs of Solomon
Practical Instructions for Successful Living

August 7

"Wrongdoers Listen To Wicked Talk; Liars Pay Attention To Destructive Words."

(Prov.17:4) NLT

"A Wicked Doer Giveth Heed To False Lips; And A Liar Giveth Ear To A Naughty Tongue."

(Prov.17:4) KJV

Proverbs of Solomon
Practical Instructions for Successful Living

August 8

Those Who Mock The Poor Insult Their Maker; Those Who Rejoice At The Misfortune Of Others Will Be Punished."

(Prov.17:5) NLT

"Whoso Mocketh The Poor Reproacheth His Maker: And He That Is Glad At Calamities Shall Not Be Unpunished."

(prov.17:5) KJV

Proverbs of Solomon
Practical Instructions for Successful Living

August 9

"Grandchildren Are The Crowning Glory Of The Aged; Parents Are The Pride Of Their Children."

(Prov.17:6) NLT

"Children's Children Are The Crown Of Old Men; And The Glory Of Children Are Their Fathers."

(Prov.17:6) KJV

Proverbs of Solomon
Practical Instructions for Successful Living

August 10

"Eloquent Speech Is Not Fitting For A Fool; Even Less Are Lies Fitting For A Ruler."

(Prov.17:7) NLT

"Excellent Speech Becometh Not A Fool: Much Less Do Lying Lips A Prince."

(Prov.17:7) KJV

Proverbs of Solomon
Practical Instructions for Successful Living

August 11

"A Bribe Seems To Work Like Magic To Those Who Give It; They Succeed In All They Do."

(Prov.17:8) NLT

"A Gift Is A Precious Stone In The Eyes Of Him That Hath It: Withersoever It Turneth, It Prospereth."

(Prov.17:8) KJV

Proverbs of Solomon
Practical Instructions for Successful Living

August 12

"Disregarding Another Person's Faults Preserves Love; Telling About Them Separates Close Friends."

(Prov.17:9) NLT

"He That Covereth A Transgression Seeketh Love; But He That Repeateth A Matter Separateth Very Friends."

(Prov.17:9) KJV

Proverbs of Solomon
Practical Instructions for Successful Living

August 13

"A Single Rebuke Does More For A Person Of Understanding Than A Hundred Lashes On The Back Of A Fool."

(Prov.17:10) NLT

"A Reproof Entereth More Into A Wise Man Than A Hundred Strips Into A Fool."

(Prov.17:10) KJV

Proverbs of Solomon
Practical Instructions for Successful Living

August 14

"Evil People Seek Rebellion, But They Will Be Severely Punished."

(Prov.17:11) NLT

"An Evil Man Seeketh Only Rebellion: Therefore A Cruel Messenger Shall Be Sent Against Him."

(Prov.17:11) KJV

Proverbs of Solomon
Practical Instructions for Successful Living

August 15

"It Is Safer To Meet A Bear Robbed Of her Cubs Than To Confront A Fool Caught In Folly."

(Prov.17:12) NLT

"Let A Bear Robbed Of Her Whelps Meet A Man, Rather Than A Fool In His Folly."

(Prov.17:12) KJV

Proverbs of Solomon
Practical Instructions for Successful Living

August 16

"If You Repay Evil For Good, Evil Will Never Leave Your House."

(Prov.17:13) NLT

"Whoso Rewardeth Evil For Good, Evil Shall Not Departeth From His House."

(Prov.17:13) KJV

Proverbs of Solomon
Practical Instructions for Successful Living

August 17

"Beginning A Quarrel Is Like Opening A Floodgate, So Drop The Matter Before A Dispute Breaks Out."

(Prov.17:14) NLT

"The Beginning Of Strife Is As When One Letteth Out Water: Therefore Leave Off Contention, Before It Be Meddled With."

(Prov.17:14) KJV

Proverbs of Solomon
Practical Instructions for Successful Living

August 18

"The LORD Despises Those Who Acquit The Guilty And Condemn The Innocent."

(Prov.17:15) NLT

"He That Justifieth The Wicked, And He That Condemneth The Just, Even They Both Are An Abomination To The LORD."

(Prov.17:16) KJV

Proverbs of Solomon
Practical Instructions for Successful Living

August 19

"A Friend Is Always Loyal, And A Brother Is Born To Help In Time Of Need."

(Prov.17:17) NLT

"A Friend Loveth At All Times, And A Brother Is Born For Adversity."

(Prov.17:17) KJV

Proverbs of Solomon
Practical Instructions for Successful Living

August 20

"It Is Poor Judgement To Co-Sign A Friends Note, To Become Responsible For A Neighbor's Debts."

(Prov.17:18) NLT

"A Man Void Of Understanding Striketh Hands, And Becometh Surety In The Presence Of His Friend."

(Prov.17:18) KJV

Proverbs of Solomon
Practical Instructions for Successful Living

August 21

"Anyone Who Loves To Quarrel Loves Sin; Anyone Who Speaks Boastful Invites Disaster."

(Prov.17:19) NLT

"He Loveth Transgression That Loveth Strife: And He That Exalteth His Gate Seeketh Destruction."

(Prov.17:19) KJV

Proverbs of Solomon
Practical Instructions for Successful Living

August 22

"The Crooked Heart Will Not Prosper; The Twisted Tongue Tumbles Into Trouble."

(Prov.17:20) NLT

"He That Hath A Froward Heart Findeth No Good: And He That Have A Perverse Tongue Falleth Into Mischief."

(Prov.17:20) KJV

Proverbs of Solomon
Practical Instructions for Successful Living

August 23

"It Is Painful To Be The Parent Of A Fool; There Is No Joy For The Father Of A Rebel."

(Prov.17:21) NLT

"He That Begetteth A Fool Doeth It To His Sorrow: And The Father Of A Fool Hath No Joy."

(Prov.17:21) KJV

Proverbs of Solomon
Practical Instructions for Successful Living

August 24

"A Cheerful Heart Is A Good Medicine, But A Broken Spirit Saps A Person's Strength."

(Prov.17:22) NLT

"A Merry Heart Doeth Good Like A Medicine: But A Broken Spirit Drieth The Bones."

(Prov.17:22) KJV

Proverbs of Solomon
Practical Instructions for Successful Living

August 25

"The Wicked Accept Secret Bribes To Pervert Justice."

(Prov.17:23) NLT

"A Wicked Man Taketh A Gift Out Of The Bosom To Pervert The Ways Of Judgment."

(Prov.17:23) KJV

Proverbs of Solomon
Practical Instructions for Successful Living

August 26

"Sensible People Keep Their Eyes Glued On Wisdom, But A Fool's Eyes Wander To The Ends Of The Earth."

(Prov.17:24) NLT

"Wisdom Is Before Him That Hath Understanding; But The Eyes Of A Fool Are In The Ends Of The Earth."

(Prov.17:24) KJV

Proverbs of Solomon
Practical Instructions for Successful Living

August 27

"Foolish Children Bring Grief To Their Father, And Bitterness To The One Who Gave Birth To Them."

(Prov.17:25) NLT

"A Foolish Son Is Grief To His Father, And Bitterness To Her That Bare Him."

(Prov.17:25) KJV

Proverbs of Solomon
Practical Instructions for Successful Living

August 28

"It Is Wrong To Find The Godly Foe Being Good Or To Punish Nobles For Being Honest!"

(Prov.17:26) NLT

"Also To Punish The Just Is Not Good, Nor To Strike Princes For Equity."

(Prov.17:26) KJV

Proverbs of Solomon
Practical Instructions for Successful Living

August 29

"A Truly Wise Person Uses Few Words; A Person With Understanding Is Even Tempered."

(Prov.17:27) NLT

"He That Hath Knowledge Spareth His words: And A Man Of Understanding Is Of An Excellent Spirit."

(Prov.17:27) KJV

Proverbs of Solomon
Practical Instructions for Successful Living

August 30

"Even Fools Are Thought To Be Wise When They Keep Silent; When They Keep Their Mouths Shut, They Seem Intelligent."

(Prov.17:28) NLT

"Even A Fool, When He Holdeth His Peace, Is Counted Wise: And He That Shutteth His Lips Is Esteemed A Man Of Understanding."

(Prov.17:28) KJV

Proverbs of Solomon
Practical Instructions for Successful Living

August 31

"A Recluse Is Self-Indulgent, Snarling At Every Sound Principle Of Conduct."

(Prov.18:1) NLT

"Through Desire A Man, Having Separated Himself, Seeketh And Intermeddleth With All Wisdom."

(Prov.18:1) KJV

Proverbs of Solomon
Practical Instructions for Successful Living

September 1

"Fools Have No Interest In Understanding; They Only Want To Air Their Opinions."

(Prov.18:2) NLT

"A Fool Hath No Delight In Understanding, But That His Heart May Discover Itself."

(Prov.18:2) KJV

Proverbs of Solomon
Practical Instructions for Successful Living

September 2

"When The Wicked Arrive, Contempt, Shame, And Disgrace Are Sure To Follow."

(Prov.18:3) NLT

"When The Wicked Cometh, Then Cometh Also Contempt, And With Ignominy Reproach."

(Prov.18:3) KJV

Proverbs of Solomon
Practical Instructions for Successful Living

September 3

"A Person's Words Can Be Life-Giving Water; Words Of True Wisdom Are As Refreshing As A Bubbling Brook."

(Prov.18:4) NLT

"The Words Of A Man's Mouth Are As Deep Waters, And The Wellspring Of Wisdom As A Flowing Brook."

(Prov.18:4) KJV

Proverbs of Solomon
Practical Instructions for Successful Living

September 4

"It Is Wrong For A Judge To Favor The Guilty Or Condemn The Innocent."

(Prov.18:5) NLT

"It Is Not Good To Accept The Person Of The Wicked, To Overthrow The Righteous In Judgement."

(Prov.18:5) KJV

Proverbs of Solomon
Practical Instructions for Successful Living

September 5

"Fools Get Into Constant Quarrels; They Are Asking For A Beating."

(Prov.18:6) NLT

"A Fools Lips Enter Into Contention, And His Mouth Calleth For Strokes."

(Prov.18:6) KJV

Proverbs of Solomon
Practical Instructions for Successful Living

September 6

"The Mouths Of Fools Are Their Ruin; Their Lips Get Them Into Trouble."

(Prov.18:7) NLT

"A Fools Mouth Is Destruction, And His Lips Are The Snare Of His Soul."

(Prov.18:7) KJV

Proverbs of Solomon
Practical Instructions for Successful Living

September 7

"What Dainty Morsel Rumors Are – But They Sink Deep Into One's Heart."

(Prov.18:8) NLT

"The Words Of A Talebearer Are As Wounds, And They Go Down Into The Innermost Parts Of The Belly."

(Prov.18:8) KJV

Proverbs of Solomon
Practical Instructions for Successful Living

September 8

"A Lazy Person Is As Bad As Someone Who Destroys Things."

(Prov.18:9) NLT

"He Also That Is Slothful In His Work Is Brother To Him That Is A Great Waster."

(Prov.18:9) KJV

Proverbs of Solomon
Practical Instructions for Successful Living

September 9

"The Name Of The LORD Is A Strong Fortress: The Godly Run To Him And Are Safe."

(Prov.18:10) NLT

"The Name Of The LORD Is A Strong Tower: The Righteous Runneth Into It, And Is Safe.

(Prov.18:10) KJV

Proverbs of Solomon
Practical Instructions for Successful Living

September 10

"The Rich Think Of Their Wealth As An Impregnable Defense; They Imagine It Is A High Wall Of Safety."

(Prov.18:11) NLT

"The Rich Man's Wealth Is His Strong City, And As A High Wall In His Own Conceit."

(Prov.18:11) KJV

Proverbs of Solomon
Practical Instructions for Successful Living

September 11

"Haughtiness Goes Before Destruction: Humility Precedes Honor."

(Prov.18:12) NLT

"Before Destruction, The Heart Of Man Is Haughty, And Before Honour Is Humility."

(Prov.18:12) KJV

Proverbs of Solomon
Practical Instructions for Successful Living

September 12

"What A Shame, What Folly, To Give Advice Before Listening To The Facts."

(Prov.18:13) NLT

"He That Answereth A Matter Before He Heareth It, It Is Folly And Shame Unto Him."

(Prov.18:13) KJV

Proverbs of Solomon
Practical Instructions for Successful Living

September 13

"The Human Spirit Can Endure A Sick Body, But Who Can Bear It If The Spirit Is Crushed."

(Prov.18:14) NLT

"The Spirit Of A Man Will Sustain His Infirmity; But A Wounded Spirit Who Can Bear."

(Prov.18:14) KJV

Proverbs of Solomon
Practical Instructions for Successful Living

September 14

"Intelligent People Are Always Open To New Ideas. In Fact They Look For Them."

(Prov.18:15) NLT

"The Heart Of The Prudent Getteth Knowledge; And The Ear Of The Wise Seeketh Knowledge."

(Prov.18:15) KJV

Proverbs of Solomon
Practical Instructions for Successful Living

September 15

"Giving A Gift Works Wonders; It May Bring You Before Important People."

(Prov.18:16) NLT

"A Man's Gift Maketh Room For Him, And Bringeth Him Before Great Men."

(Prov.18:16) KJV

Proverbs of Solomon
Practical Instructions for Successful Living

September 16

"Any Story Sounds True Until Someone Sets The Record Straight."

(Prov.18:17) NLT

"He That Is First In His Own Cause Seemeth Just; But His Neighbor Cometh And Searcheth Him."

(Prov.18:17) KJV

Proverbs of Solomon
Practical Instructions for Successful Living

September 17

"Casting Lots Can End Arguments And Settle Disputes Between Powerful Opponents."

(Prov.18:18) NLT

"The Lot Causeth Contentions To Cease, And Parteth Between The Mighty."

(Prov.18:18) KJV

Proverbs of Solomon
Practical Instructions for Successful Living

September 18

"It's Harder To Make Amends With An Offended Friend Than To Capture A Fortified City. Arguments Separate Friends Like A Gate Locked With Iron Bars."

(Prov.18:19) NLT

"A Brother Offended Is Harder To Be Won Than A Strong City: And Their Contentions Are Like The Bars Of A Castle."

(Prov.18:19) KJV

Proverbs of Solomon
Practical Instructions for Successful Living

September 19

"Works Satisfy The Soul As Food Satisfies The Stomach; The Right Words On A Person's Lips Bring Satisfaction."

(Prov.18:20) NLT

"A Man's Belly Shall Be Satisfied With The Fruit Of His Mouth; And With The Increase Of His Lips Shall He Be Filled."

(Prov.18:20) KJV

Proverbs of Solomon
Practical Instructions for Successful Living

September 20

"Those Who Love To Talk Will Experience The Consequences, For The Tongue Can Kill Or Nourish Life."

(Prov.18:21) NLT

"Death And Life Are In The Power Of The Tongue: And They That Love It Shall Eat The Fruit Thereof."

(Prov.18:21) KJV

Proverbs of Solomon
Practical Instructions for Successful Living

September 21

"The Man Who Finds A Wife Finds A Treasure And Receives Favor From The LORD."

(Prov.18:22) NLT

"Whoso Findeth A Wife Findeth A Good Thing, And Obtaineth Favour Of the LORD."

(Prov.18:22) KJV

Proverbs of Solomon
Practical Instructions for Successful Living

September 22

"The Poor Plead For Mercy; The Rich Answer With Insults."

(Prov.18:23) NLT

"The Poor Useth Intreaties; But The Rich Answereth Roughly."

(Prov.18:23) KJV

Proverbs of Solomon
Practical Instructions for Successful Living

September 23

"There Are "Friends" Who Destroy Each Other, But A Real Friend Sticks Closer Than A Brother."

(Prov.18:24) NLT

"A Man That Hath Friends Must Shew Himself Friendly: And There Is A Friend That Sticketh Closer Than A Brother."

(Prov.18:24) KJV

Proverbs of Solomon
Practical Instructions for Successful Living

September 24

"It Is Better To Be Poor And Honest Than To Be A Fool And Dishonest."

(Prov.19:1) NLT

"Better Is The Poor That Walketh In His Integrity, Than He That Is Perverse In His Lips, And Is A Fool."

(Prov.19:1) KJV

Proverbs of Solomon
Practical Instructions for Successful Living

September 25

"Zeal Without Knowledge Is Not Good; A Person Who Moves Too Quickly May Go The Wrong Way."

(Prov.19:2) NLT

"Also, That The Soul Be Without Knowledge, It Is Not Good; And He Hath Hasteth With His Feet Sinneth."

(Prov.19:2) KJV

Proverbs of Solomon
Practical Instructions for Successful Living

September 26

"People Ruin Their Lives By Their Own Foolishness And Then Are Angry At The LORD."

(Prov.19:3) NLT

"The Foolishness Of Man Perverteth His Way: And His Heart Fretteth Against The LORD."

(Prov.19:3) KJV

Proverbs of Solomon
Practical Instructions for Successful Living

September 27

"Wealth Makes Many "Friends"; Poverty Drives Them Away."

(Prov.19:4) NLT

"Wealth Maketh Many Friends; But The Poor Is Separated From His Neighbour."

(Prov.19:4) KJV

Proverbs of Solomon
Practical Instructions for Successful Living

September 28

"A False Witness Will Not Go Unpunished, Nor Will A Liar Escape."

(Prov.19:5) NLT

"A False Witness Shall Not Be Unpunished, And He That Speaketh Lies Shall Not Escape."

(Prov.19:5) KJV

Proverbs of Solomon
Practical Instructions for Successful Living

September 29

"Many Beg Favors From A Prince; Everyone Is The Friend Of A Person Who Gives Gifts."

(Prov.19:6) NLT

"Many Will Intreat The Favour Of The Prince: And Every Man Is A Friend To Him That Giveth Gifts."

(Prov.19:6) KJV

Proverbs of Solomon
Practical Instructions for Successful Living

September 30

"If The Relative Of The Poor Despise Them, How Much More Will Their Friends Avoid Them. The Poor Call After Them, But They Are Gone."

(Prov.19:7) NLT

"All The Brethren Of The Poor Do Hate Him: How Much More Do His Friends Go Far From Him? He Pursueth Them With Words, Yet They Are Wanting To Him."

(Prov.19:7) KJV

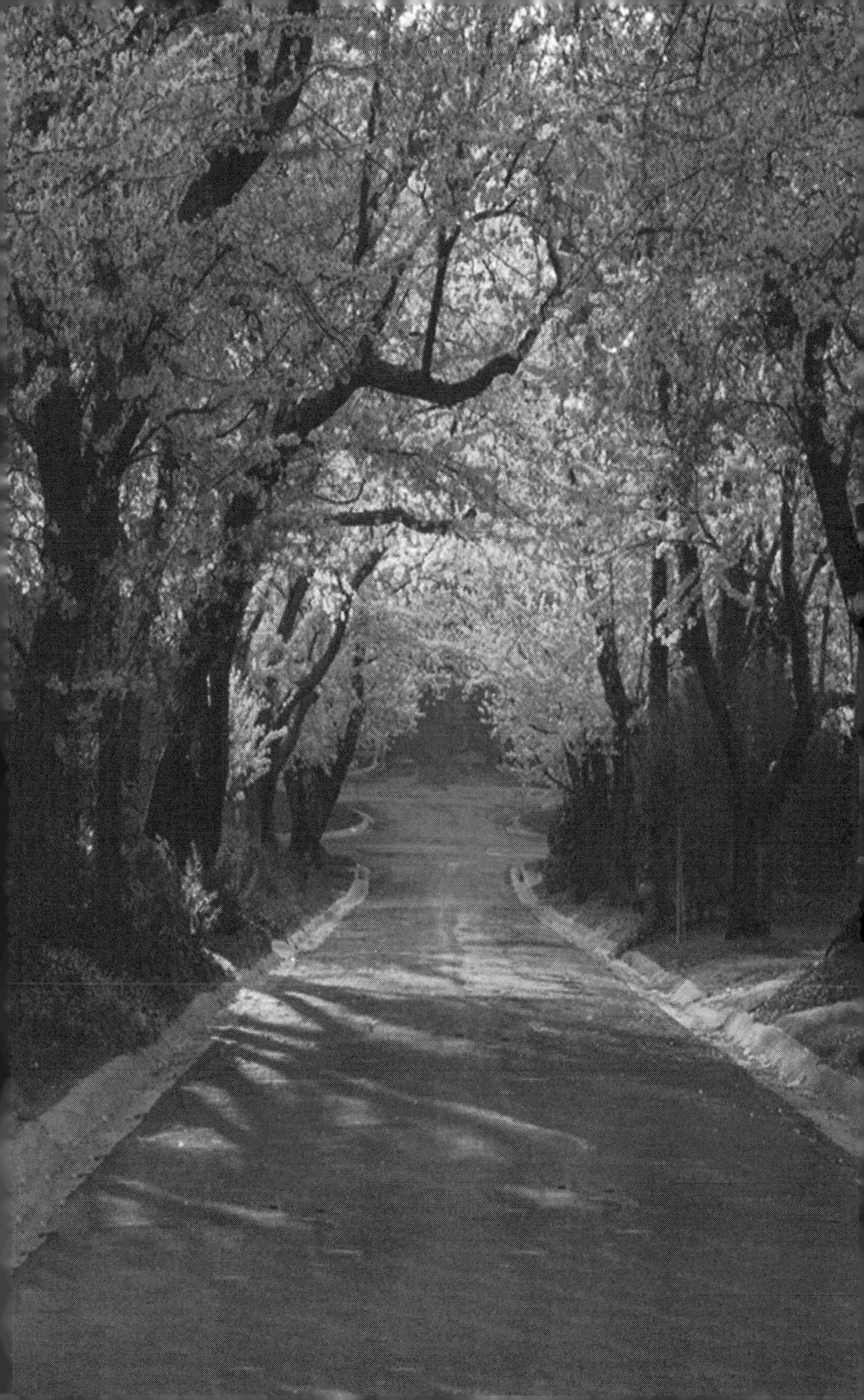

Proverbs of Solomon
Practical Instructions for Successful Living

October 1

"To Acquire Wisdom Is To Love Oneself; People Who Cherish Understanding Will Prosper."

(Prov.19:8) NLT

"He That Getteth Wisdom Loveth His Own Soul: He That Keepeth Understanding Shall Find Good."

(Prov.19:8) KJV

Proverbs of Solomon
Practical Instructions for Successful Living

October 2

"A False Witness Will Not Go Unpunished, And A Liar Will Be Destroyed."

(Prov.19:9) NLT

"A False Witness Shall Not Be Unpunished, And He That Speaketh Lies Shall Perish."

(Prov.19:9)

Proverbs of Solomon
Practical Instructions for Successful Living

October 3

"It Isn't Right For A Fool To Live In Luxury Or For A Slave to Rule Over Princes."

(Prov.19:10) NLT

"Delight Is Not Seemly For A Fool; Much Less For A Servant To Have Rule Over Princes."

(Prov.19:10) KJV

Proverbs of Solomon
Practical Instructions for Successful Living

October 4

"People With Good Sense Restrain Their Anger; They Earn Esteem By Overlooking Wrongs."

(Prov.19:11) NLT

"The Discretion Of A Man Deferreth His Anger; And It Is His Glory To Pass Over A Transgression."

(Prov.19:11) KJV

Proverbs of Solomon
Practical Instructions for Successful Living

October 5

"The King's Anger Is Like A Lion's Roar, But His Favor Is Like Dew On The Grass."

(Prov.19:12) NLT

"The King's Wrath Is As The Roaring Of A Lion; But His Favour Is As Dew Upon The Grass."

(Prov.19:12) KJV

Proverbs of Solomon
Practical Instructions for Successful Living

October 6

"A Foolish Child Is A Calamity To A Father; A Nagging Wife Annoys Like A Constant Dripping."

(Prov.19:13) NLT

"A Foolish Son Is The Calamity Of His Father: And The Contentions Of A Wife Are A Continual Dripping."

(Prov.19:13) KJV

Proverbs of Solomon
Practical Instructions for Successful Living

October 7

"Parents Can Provide Their Sons With An Inheritance Of Houses And Wealth, But Only The LORD Can Give An Understanding Wife."

(Prov.19:14) NLT

"House And Riches Are The Inheritance Of Fathers: And A Prudent Wife Is From The LORD."

(Prov.19:14) KJV

Proverbs of Solomon
Practical Instructions for Successful Living

October 8

"A Lazy Person Sleeps Soundly – And Goes Hungry."

(Prov.19:15) NLT

"Slothfulness Casteth Into A Deep Sleep; And An Idle Soul Shall Suffer Hunger."

(Prov.19:15) KJV

Proverbs of Solomon
Practical Instructions for Successful Living

October 9

"Keep The Commandments And Keep Your Life; Despising Them Leads To Death."

(Prov.19:16) NLT

"He That Keepeth The Commandment Keepeth His Own Soul; But He That Despiseth His Ways Shall Die."

(Prov.19:16) KJV

Proverbs of Solomon
Practical Instructions for Successful Living

October 10

"If You Help The Poor, You Are Lending To The LORD – And He Will Repay You."

(Prov.19:17) NLT

"He That Hath Pity Upon The Poor Lendeth Unto The LORD; And That Which He Hath Given Will He Pay Him Again."

(Prov.19:17) KJV

Proverbs of Solomon
Practical Instructions for Successful Living

October 11

"Discipline Your Children While There Is Hope. If You Don't, You Will Ruin Their Lives."

(Prov.19:18) NLT

"Chasten Thy Son While There Is Hope, And Let Not Thy Soul Spare For His Crying."

(Prov.19:18) KJV

Proverbs of Solomon
Practical Instructions for Successful Living

October 12

"Short-Tempered People Must Pay Their Own Penalty. If You Rescue Them Once, You Will Have To Do It Again."

(Prov.19:19) NLT

"A Man Of Great Wrath Shall Suffer Punishment: For If Thou Deliver Him, Yet Thou Must Do It Again."

(Prov.19:19) KJV

Proverbs of Solomon
Practical Instructions for Successful Living

October 13

"Get All The Advice And Instruction You Can, And Be Wise The Rest Of Your Life."

(Prov.19:20) NLT

"Hear Counsel, And Receive Instruction, That Thou Mayest Be Wise In Thy Latter End."

(Prov.19:20) KJV

Proverbs of Solomon
Practical Instructions for Successful Living

October 14

"You Can Make Many Plans, But The LORD'S Purpose Will Prevail."

(Prov.19:21) NLT

"There Are Many Devices In A Man's Heart; Nevertheless The Counsel Of The LORD, That Shall Stand."

(Prov.19:21) KJV

Proverbs of Solomon
Practical Instructions for Successful Living

October 15

"Loyalty Makes A Person Attractive. And It Is Better To Be Poor Than Dishonest."

(Prov.19:22) NLT

"The Desire Of A Man Is His Kindness: And A Poor Man Is Better Than A Liar."

(Prov.19:22) KJV

Proverbs of Solomon
Practical Instructions for Successful Living

October 16

"Fear Of The LORD Gives Life, Security, And Protection From Harm."

(Prov.19:23) NLT

"The Fear Of The LORD Tendeth To Life: And He That Hath It Shall Abide Satisfied: He Shall Not Be Visited With Evil."

(Prov.19:23) KJV

Proverbs of Solomon
Practical Instructions for Successful Living

October 17

"Some People Are So Lazy That They Won't Even Lift A Finger To Feed Themselves."

(Prov.19:24) NLT

"A Slothful Man Hideth His Hand In His Bosom, And Will Not So Much As Bring It To His Mouth Again."

(Prov.19:24) KJV

Proverbs of Solomon
Practical Instructions for Successful Living

October 18

"If You Punish A Mocker, The Simpleminded Will Learn A Lesson; If You Reprove The Wise, They Will Be All The Wiser."

(Prov.19:25) NLT

"Smite A Scorner, And The Simple Will Beware: And Reprove One That Hath Understanding, And He Will Understand Knowledge."

(Prov.19:25) KJV

Proverbs of Solomon
Practical Instructions for Successful Living

October 19

"Children Who Mistreat Their Father Or Chase Away Their Mother Are A Public Disgrace And Embarrassment."

(Prov.19:26) NLT

"He That Wasteth His Father, And Chaseth Away His Mother, Is A Son That Causeth Shame, And Bringeth Reproach."

(Prov.19:26) KJV

Proverbs of Solomon
Practical Instructions for Successful Living

October 20

"If You Stop Listening To Instruction, My Child, You Have Turned Your Back On Knowledge."

(Prov.19:27) NLT

"Cease, My Son, To Hear The Instruction That Causeth To Err From The Words Of Knowledge."

(Prov.19:27) KJV

Proverbs of Solomon
Practical Instructions for Successful Living

October 21

"A Corrupt Witness Makes A Mockery Of Justice; The Mouth Of The Wicked Gulps Down Evil."

(Prov.19:28) NLT

"An Ungodly Witness Scorneth Judgment: And The Mouth Of The Wicked Devoureth Iniquity."

(Prov.19:28) KJV

Proverbs of Solomon
Practical Instructions for Successful Living

October 22

"Mockers Will Be Punished, And The Backs Of Fools Will Be Beaten."

(Prov.19:29) NLT

"Judgments Are Prepared For Scorners, And Stripes For The Backs Of Fools."

(Prov.19:29) KJV

Proverbs of Solomon
Practical Instructions for Successful Living

October 23

"Wine Produces Mockers; Liquor Leads To Brawls. Whoever Is Lead Astray by Drink Cannot Be Wise."

(Prov.20:1) NLT

"Wine Is A Mocker, Strong Drink Is Raging: And Whosoever Is Deceived Thereby Is Not Wise."

(Prov.20:1) KJV

Proverbs of Solomon
Practical Instructions for Successful Living

October 24

"The King's Fury Is Like A Lion's Roar; To Rouse His Anger Is To Risk Your Life."

(Prov.20:2) NLT

"The Fear Of A King Is As The Roaring Of A Lion: Whoso Provoketh Him To Anger Sinneth Against His Own Soul."

(Prov.20:2) KJV

Proverbs of Solomon
Practical Instructions for Successful Living

October 25

"Avoiding A Fight Is A Mark Of Honor; Only Fools Insist On Quarreling."

(Prov.20:3) NLT

"Is Honour For A Man To Cease From Strife: But Every Fool Will Be Meddling."

(Prov.20:3) KJV

Proverbs of Solomon
Practical Instructions for Successful Living

October 26

"If You Are Too Lazy To Plow In The Right Season, You Will Have No Food At The Harvest."

(Prov.20:4) NLT

"The Sluggard Will Not Plow By Reason Of The cold; Therefore Shall He Beg In Harvest, And Have Nothing."

(Prov.20:4) KJV

Proverbs of Solomon
Practical Instructions for Successful Living

October 27

"Though Good Advice Lies Deep Within A Person's Heart, The Wise Will Draw Out."

(Prov.20:5) NLT

"Counsel In The Heart Of Man Is Like Deep Water; But A Man Of Understanding Will Draw It Out."

(Prov.20:5) KJV

Proverbs of Solomon
Practical Instructions for Successful Living

October 28

"Many Will Say They Are Loyal Friends, But Who Can Find One That Is Really Faithful?"

(Prov.20:6) NLT

"Most Men Will Proclaim Every One His Own Goodness: But A Faithful Man Who Can Find?"

(Prov.20:6) KJV

Proverbs of Solomon
Practical Instructions for Successful Living

October 29

"The Godly Walk With Integrity: Blessed Are Their Children Who Follow Them."

(Prov.20:7) NLT

"The Just Man Walketh In His Integrity: His Children Are Blessed After Him."

(Prov.20:7) KJV

Proverbs of Solomon
Practical Instructions for Successful Living

October 30

"When A King Judges, He Carefully Weighs All The Evidence, Distinguishing The Bad From The Good."

(Prov.20:8) NLT

"A King That Sitteth In The Throne Of Judgment Scattereth Away All Evil With His Eyes."

(Prov.20:8) KJV

Proverbs of Solomon
Practical Instructions for Successful Living

October 31

Who Can Say, "I Have Cleansed My Heart; I Am Pure And Free From Sin?"

(Prov.20:9) NLT

Who Can Say," I Have Made My Heart Clean, I Am Pure From My Sin?"

(Prov.20:9) KJV

Proverbs of Solomon
Practical Instructions for Successful Living

November 1

"The LORD Despises Double Standards Of Every Kind."

(Prov.20:10) NLT

"Divers Weights, And Divers Measures, Both Of Them Are Alike Abomination To The LORD."

(Prov.20:10) KJV

Proverbs of Solomon
Practical Instructions for Successful Living

November 2

"Even Children Are Known By The Way They Act, Whether Their Conduct Is Pure And Right."

(Prov.20:11) NLT

"Even A Child Is Known By His Doings, Whether His Work Be Pure, And Whether It Be Right."

(Prov.20:11) KJV

Proverbs of Solomon
Practical Instructions for Successful Living

November 3

"Ears To Hear And Eyes To See – Both Are Gifts From The LORD."

(Prov.20:12) NLT

"The Hearing Ear, And The Seeing Eye, The LORD Hath Made Even Both Of Them."

(Prov.20:12) KJV

Proverbs of Solomon
Practical Instructions for Successful Living

November 4

"If You Sleep, You Will End In Poverty. Keep Your Eyes Open, And There Will Be Plenty To Eat."

(Prov.20:13) NLT

"Love Not Sleep, Lest Thou Come To Poverty; Open Thine Eyes, And Thou Shalt Be Satisfied With Bread."

(Prov.20:13) KJV

Proverbs of Solomon
Practical Instructions for Successful Living

November 5

"The Buyer Haggles Over The Price, Saying, "It's Worthless." Then Brags About Getting A Bargain!"

(Prov.20:14) NLT

"It Is Naught, It Is Naught, Saith The Buyer: But When He Is Gone His Way, Then He Boasteth."

(Prov.20:14) KJV

Proverbs of Solomon
Practical Instructions for Successful Living

November 6

"Wise Speech Is Rarer And More Valuable than Gold And Rubies."

(Prov.20:15) NLT

"There Is Gold, And A Multitude Of Rubies: But The Lips Of Knowledge Are A Precious Jewel."

(Prov.20:15) KJV

Proverbs of Solomon
Practical Instructions for Successful Living

November 7

"Be Sure To Get Collateral From Anyone Who Guarantees The Debt Of A Stranger. Get A Deposit If Someone Guaranteed The Debt Of A Foreigner."

(Prov.20:16) NLT

"Take His Garment That Is Surety For A Stranger: And Take A Pledge Of Him For A Strange Woman."

(Prov.20:16) KJV

Proverbs of Solomon
Practical Instructions for Successful Living

November 8

"Stolen Bread Tastes Sweet, But It Turns To Gravel In The Mouth."

(Prov.20:17) NLT

"Bread Of Deceit Is Sweet To A Man; But Afterwards His Mouth Shall Be Filled With Gravel."

(Prov.20:17) KJV

Proverbs of Solomon
Practical Instructions for Successful Living

November 9

"Plans Succeed Through Good Counsel; Don't Go To War Without The Advice Of Others."

(Prov.20:18) NLT

"Every Purpose Is Established By Counsel: And With Good Advice Make War."

(Prov.20:18) KJV

Proverbs of Solomon
Practical Instructions for Successful Living

November 10

"A Gossip Tells Secrets, So Don't Hang Around With Someone Who Talks Too Much."

(Prov.20:19) NLT

"He That Goeth About As A Tale Bearer Revealeth Secrets: Therefore Meddle Not With Him That Flattereth With His Lips."

(Prov.20:19) KJV

Proverbs of Solomon
Practical Instructions for Successful Living

November 11

"If You Curse Your Father Or Mother, The Lamp Of Your Life Will Be Snuffed Out."

(Prov.20:20) NLT

"Whoso Curseth His Father Or His Mother, His Lamp Shall Be Put Out In Obscure Darkness."

(Prov.20:20) KJV

Proverbs of Solomon
Practical Instructions for Successful Living

November 12

"An Inheritance Obtained Early In Life Is Not A Blessing In The End."

(Prov.20:21) NLT

"An Inheritance May Be Gotten Hastily At The Beginning; But The End Thereof Shall Not Be Blessed."

(Prov.20:21) KJV

Proverbs of Solomon
Practical Instructions for Successful Living

November 13

"Don't Say, "I Will Get Even For This Wrong." Wait For the LORD To Handle This Matter."

(Prov.20:22) NLT

"Say Not Thou, I Will Recompense Evil; But Wait On The LORD, And He Shall Save Thee."

(Prov.20:22) KJV

Proverbs of Solomon
Practical Instructions for Successful Living

November 14

"The LORD Despises Double Standards; He Is Not Pleased By Dishonest Scales."

(Prov.20:23) NLT

"Divers Weights Are An Abomination Unto The LORD; And A False Balance Is Not Good."

(Prov.20:23) KJV

Proverbs of Solomon
Practical Instructions for Successful Living

November 15

"How Can We Understand The Road We Travel? It Is The LORD Who Directs Our Steps."

(Prov.20:24) NLT

"Man's Goings Are Of the LORD; How Can A Man Then Understand His Own Way?"

(Prov.20:24) KJV

Proverbs of Solomon
Practical Instructions for Successful Living

November 16

"It Is Dangerous To Make A Rash Promise To God Before Counting The Cost."

(Prov.20:25) NLT

"It Is A Snare To The Man Who Devoureth That Which Is Holy, And After Vows To Make Inquiry."

(Prov.20:25) KJV

Proverbs of Solomon
Practical Instructions for Successful Living

November 17

"A Wise King Finds The Wicked, Lays Them Out Like Wheat, Then Runs The Crushing Wheel Over Them."

(Prov.20:26) NLT

"A Wise King Scattereth The Wicked, And Bringeth The Wheel Over Them."

(Prov.20:26) KJV

Proverbs of Solomon
Practical Instructions for Successful Living

November 18

"The LORD's Searchlight Penetrates The Human Spirit, Exposing Every Hidden Motive."

(Prov.20:27) NLT

"The Spirit Of Man Is The Candle Of The LORD, Searching All The Inward Parts Of The Belly."

(Prov.20:27) KJV

Proverbs of Solomon
Practical Instructions for Successful Living

November 19

"Unfailing Love And Faithfulness Protect The King; His Throne Is Made Secure Through Love."

(Prov.20:28) NLT

"Mercy And Truth Preserve The King: And His Throne Is Upholden By Mercy."

(Prov.20:28) KJV

Proverbs of Solomon
Practical Instructions for Successful Living

November 20

"The Glory Of The Young Is their Strength; The Gray Hair Of Experience Is The Splendor Of The Old."

(Prov.20:29) NLT

"The Glory Of Young Men Is Their Strength: And The Beauty Of Old Men Is The Gray Head."

(Prov.20:29) KJV

Proverbs of Solomon
Practical Instructions for Successful Living

November 21

"Physical Punishment Cleanses Away Evil; Such Discipline Purifies The Heart."

(Prov.20:30) NLT

"The Blueness Of A Wound Cleanseth Away Evil: So Do Stripes The Inward Parts Of The Belly."

(Prov.20:30) KJV

Proverbs of Solomon
Practical Instructions for Successful Living

November 22

"The King's Heart Is Like A Stream Of Water Directed By The LORD; He Turns It Wherever He Pleases."

(Prov.21:1) NLT

"The King's Heart Is In The Hand Of The LORD, As The Rivers Of Water: He Turneth It Whithersoever He Will."

(Prov.21:1) KJV

Proverbs of Solomon
Practical Instructions for Successful Living

November 23

"People May Think They Are Doing What Is Right, But The LORD Examines The Heart."

(Prov.21:2) NLT

"Every Way Of A Man Is Right In His Own Eyes: But The LORD Pondereth The Hearts."

(Prov.21:2) KJV

Proverbs of Solomon
Practical Instructions for Successful Living

November 24

"The LORD Is More Pleased When We Do What Is Right Than When We Give Him Sacrifices."

(Prov.21:3) NLT

"To Do Justice And Judgment Is More Acceptable To The LORD Than Sacrifice."

(Prov.21:3) KJV

Proverbs of Solomon
Practical Instructions for Successful Living

November 25

"Haughty Eyes, A Proud Heart, And Evil Actions Are All Sin."

(Prov.21:4) NLT

"An High Look, And A Proud Heart, And The Plowing Of The Wicked, Is Sin."

(Prov.21:4) KJV

Proverbs of Solomon
Practical Instructions for Successful Living

November 26

"Good Planning And Hard Work Lead To Prosperity, But Hasty Shortcuts Lead To Poverty."

(Prov.21:5) NLT

"The Thoughts Of The Diligent Tend Only To Plenteousness; But Of Every One That Is Hasty Only To Want."

(Prov.21:5) KJV

Proverbs of Solomon
Practical Instructions for Successful Living

November 27

"Wealth Created By Lying Is A Vanishing Mist And A Deadly Trap."

(Prov.21:6) NLT

"The Getting Of Treasures By A Lying Tongue Is A Vanity Tossed To And Fro Of Them That Seek Death."

(Prov.21:6) KJV

Proverbs of Solomon
Practical Instructions for Successful Living

November 28

"Because The Wicked Refuse To Do What Is Just, Their Violence Boomerangs And Destroys Them."

(Prov.21:7) NLT

"The Robbery Of The Wicked Shall Destroy Them; Because They Refuse To Do Judgment."

(Prov.21:7) KJV

Proverbs of Solomon
Practical Instructions for Successful Living

November 29

"The Guilty Walk A Crooked Path; The Innocent Travel A Straight Road."

(Prov.21:8) NLT

"The Way Of Man Is Froward And Strange: But As For The Pure, His Work Is Right."

(Prov.21:8) KJV

Proverbs of Solomon
Practical Instructions for Successful Living

November 30

"It Is Better To Live Alone In The Corner Of An Attic Than With A Contentious Wife In A Lovely Home."

(Prov.21:9) NLT

"It Is Better To Dwell In The Corner Of The Housetop, Than With A Brawling Woman In A Wide House."

(Prov.21:9) KJV

Proverbs of Solomon
Practical Instructions for Successful Living

December 1

"Evil People Love To Harm Others; Their Neighbors Get No Mercy From Them."

(Prov.21:10) NLT

"The Soul Of The Wicked Desireth Evil: His Neighbour Findeth No Favour In His Eyes."

(Prov.21:10) KV

Proverbs of Solomon
Practical Instructions for Successful Living

December 2

"A Simpleton Can Learn Only By Seeing Mockers Punished; A Wise Person Learns From Instruction."

(Prov.21:11) NLT

"When The Scorner Is Punished, The Simple Is Made Wise: And When The Wise Is Instructed, He Receiveth Knowledge."

(Prov.21:11) KJV

Proverbs of Solomon
Practical Instructions for Successful Living

December 3

"The Righteous One Knows What Is Going On In The Homes Of The Wicked; He Will Bring The Wicked To Disaster."

(Prov.21:12) NLT

"The Righteous Man Wisely Considereth The House Of The Wicked: But God Overthroweth The Wicked For Their Wickedness."

(Prov.21:12) KJV

Proverbs of Solomon
Practical Instructions for Successful Living

December 4

"Those Who Shut Their Ears To The Cries Of The Poor Will Be Ignore In Their Own Time Of Need."

(Prov.21:13) NLT

"Whoso Stoppeth His Ears At The Cry Of The Poor, He Also Shall Cry Himself, But Shall Not Be Heard."

(Prov.21:13) KJV

Proverbs of Solomon
Practical Instructions for Successful Living

December 5

"A Secret Gift Calms Anger; A Secret Bribe Pacifies Fury."

(Prov.21:14) NLT

"A Gift In Secret Pacifieth Anger: And A Reward In The Bosom Strong Wrath."

(Prov.21:14) KJV

Proverbs of Solomon
Practical Instructions for Successful Living

December 6

"Justice Is A Joy To The Godly, But It Causes Dismay Among Evildoers."

(Prov.21:15) NLT

"It Is Joy To The Just To Do Judgment: But Destruction Shall Be To The Workers Of Iniquity."

(Prov.21:15) KJV

Proverbs of Solomon
Practical Instructions for Successful Living

December 7

"The Person Who Strays From Common Sense Will End Up In The Company Of The Dead."

(Prov.21:16) NLT

"The Man That Wandereth Out Of The Way Of Understanding Shall Remain In The Congregation Of The Dead."

(Prov.21:16) KJV

Proverbs of Solomon
Practical Instructions for Successful Living

December 8

"Those Who Love Pleasure Become Poor; Wine And Luxury Are Not The Way To Riches."

(Prov.21:17) NLT

"He That Loveth Pleasure Shall Be A Poor Man: He That Loveth Wine And Oil Shall Not Be Rich."

(Pdrov.21:17) KJV

Proverbs of Solomon
Practical Instructions for Successful Living

December 9

"Sometimes The Wicked Are Punished To Save The Godly, And The Treacherous For The Upright."

(Prov.21:18) NLT

"The Wicked Shall Be A Ransom For The Righteous, And The Transgressor For The Upright."

(Prov.21:18) KJV

Proverbs of Solomon
Practical Instructions for Successful Living

December 10

"It Is Better To Live Alone In The Desert Than With A Crabby, Complaining Wife."

(Prov.21:19) NLT

"It Is Better To Dwell In The Wilderness, Than With A Contentious And An Angry Woman."

(Prov.21:19) KJV

Proverbs of Solomon
Practical Instructions for Successful Living

December 11

"The Wise Have Wealth And Luxury, But Fools Spend Whatever They Get."

(Prov.21:20) NLT

"There Is Treasure To Be Desired And Oil In The Dwelling Of The Wise; But A Foolish Man Spendeth It Up."

(Prov.21:20) KJV

Proverbs of Solomon
Practical Instructions for Successful Living

December 12

"Whoever Pursues Godliness And Unfailing Love Will Find Life, Godliness, And Honor."

(Prov.21:21) NLT

"He That Followeth After Righteousness And Mercy Findeth Life, Righteousness, And Honour."

(Prov.21:21) KJV

Proverbs of Solomon
Practical Instructions for Successful Living

December 13

"The Wise Conquer The City Of The Strong And Level The Fortress In Which They Trust."

(Prov.21:22) NLT

"A Wise Man Scaleth The City Of The Mighty, And Casteth Down the Strength Of The Confidence Thereof."

(Prov.21:22) KJV

Proverbs of Solomon
Practical Instructions for Successful Living

December 14

"If You Keep Your Mouth Shut, You Will Stay Out Of Trouble."

(Prov.21:23) NLT

"Whoso Keepeth His Mouth And His Tongue Keepeth His Soul From Troubles."

(Prov.21:23) KJV

Proverbs of Solomon
Practical Instructions for Successful Living

December 15

"Mockers Are Proud And Haughty; They Act With Boundless Arrogance."

(Prov.21:24) NLT

"Proud And Haughty Scorner Is His Name, Who Dealeth In Proud Wrath."

(Prov.21:24) KJV

Proverbs of Solomon
Practical Instructions for Successful Living

December 16

"The Desires Of Lazy People Will Be Their Ruin, For Their Hands Refuse To Work."

(Prov.21:25) NLT

"The Desire Of The Slothful Killeth Him; For His Hands Refuse To Labour."

(Prov.21:25) KJV

Proverbs of Solomon
Practical Instructions for Successful Living

December 17

"They Are Always Greedy For More, While The Godly Love To Give!"

(Prov.21:26) NLT

"He Coveteth Greedily All The Day Long; But The Righteous Giveth And Spareth Not."

(Prov.21:26) KJV

Proverbs of Solomon
Practical Instructions for Successful Living

December 18

"God Loathes The Sacrifice Of An Evil Person, Especially When It Is Brought With Ulterior Motives."

(Prov.21:27) NLT

"The Sacrifice Of The Wicked Is Abomination: How Much More, When He Bringeth It With A Wicked Mind?"

(Prov.21:27) KJV

Proverbs of Solomon
Practical Instructions for Successful Living

December 19

"A False Witness Will Be Cut Off, But An Attentive Witness Will Be Allowed To Speak."

(Prov.21:28) NLT

"A False Witness Shall Perish: But The Man That Heareth Speaketh Constantly."

(Prov.21:28) KJV

Proverbs of Solomon
Practical Instructions for Successful Living

December 20

"The Wicked Put Up A Bold Front, But The Upright Proceed With Care."

(Prov.21:29) NLT

"A Wicked Man Hardeneth His Face: But As For The Upright, He Directeth His Way."

(Prov.21:29) KJV

Proverbs of Solomon
Practical Instructions for Successful Living

December 21

"Human Plans, No Matter How Wise Or Well Advised, Cannot Stand Against The LORD."

(Prov.21:30) NLT

"There Is No Wisdom Nor Understanding Nor Counsel Against The LORD."

(Prov.21:30) KJV

Proverbs of Solomon
Practical Instructions for Successful Living

December 22

"The Horses Are Prepared For Battle, But The Victory Belongs To The LORD."

(Prov.21:31) NLT

"The Horse Is Prepared Against The Day Of Battle: But Safety Is Of The LORD."

(Prov.21:31) KJV

Proverbs of Solomon
Practical Instructions for Successful Living

December 23

"Choose A Good Reputation Over Great Riches, For Being Held In High Esteem Is Better Than Having Silver Or Gold."

(Prov.22:1) NLT

"A Good Name Is Rather To Be Chosen Than Great Riches, And Loving Favour Rather Than Silver And Gold."

(Prov.22:1) KJV

Proverbs of Solomon
Practical Instructions for Successful Living

December 24

"The Rich And The Poor Have This In Common: The LORD Made Them Both."

(Prov.22:2) NLT

"The Rich And The Poor Meet Together: The LORD Is Maker Of Them All."

(Prov.22:2) KJV

Proverbs of Solomon
Practical Instructions for Successful Living

December 25

"A Prudent Person Sees The Danger Ahead And Takes Precautions; The Simpleton Goes Blindly On And Suffers The Consequences."

(Prov.22:3) NLT

"A Prudent Man Foreseeth The Evil, And Hideth Himself: But The Simple Pass On, And Are Punished."

(Prov.22:3) KJV

Proverbs of Solomon
Practical Instructions for Successful Living

December 26

"True Humility And Fear Of The LORD Lead To Riches, Honor, And Long Life."

(Prov.22:4) NLT

"By Humility And The Fear Of The LORD Are Riches, And Honour, And Life."

(Prov.22:4) KJV

Proverbs of Solomon
Practical Instructions for Successful Living

December 27

"The Deceitful Walk A Thorny, Treacherous Road; Whoever Values Life Will Stay Away."

(Prov.22:5) NLT

"Thorns And Snares Are In The Way Of The Froward: He That Doth Keep His Soul Shall Be Far From Them."

(Prov.22:5) KJV

Proverbs of Solomon
Practical Instructions for Successful Living

December 28

"Teach Your Children To Choose the Right Path, And When They Are Older, They Will Remain Upon It."

(Prov.22:6) NLT

"Train Up A Child In The Way He Should Go: An When He Is Old, He Will Not Depart From It."

(Prov.22:6) KJV

Proverbs of Solomon
Practical Instructions for Successful Living

December 29

"Just As The Rich Rule The Poor, So The Borrower Is Servant To The Lender."

(Prov.22:7) NLT

"The Rich Ruleth Over The Poor, And The Borrower Is Servant To The Lender."

(Prov.22:7) KJV

Proverbs of Solomon
Practical Instructions for Successful Living

December 30

"Those Who Plant Seeds Of Injustice Will Harvest Disaster, And Their Reign Of Terror Will End."

(Prov.22:8) NLT

"He That Soweth Iniquity Shall Reap Vanity: And The Rod Of His Anger Shall Fail."

(Prov.22:8) KJV

Proverbs of Solomon
Practical Instructions for Successful Living

December 31

"Blessed Are Those Who Are Generous, Because They Feed The Poor."

(Prov.22:9) NLT

"He That Hath A Bountiful Eye Shall Be Blessed; For He Giveth Of His Bread to The Poor."

(Prov.22:9) KJV

ABOUT THE AUTHOR

Ever since she was a little girl, Bridgett has been seeking GOD, wanting to satisfy her hunger and thirst for knowledge, wisdom and understanding of GOD'S Word and HIS Way. GOD has taken Bridgett's love for HIM, reading, and writing and is Purposing her to become an Author/Transcriber of The Word of GOD, not only through her, but through different men and women of GOD, Servants, and Kingdom Builders, in this Earthly realm. "The Proverbs Of Solomon..." is the first in a series of books to be released, in GOD'S Time. Bridgett Muldrow was born the 14th of October during 1969 in Springfield, Massachusetts to William "Ted" and Almond (Martin) Muldrow: May They Rest In Peace. In 1998, Bridgett later relocated to Atlanta, Georgia, where her Spirituality became clearer, and the vision for this book and future books came to her.

Made in the USA
Columbia, SC
07 June 2024

9b748678-f9d5-4aaf-84d4-3fd828ff63d8R01